Presented to

_____

By

_____

On the Occasion of

_____

Date

_____

THE PRAYER OF JESUS

*Developing Intimacy
with God through
Christ's Example*

MIKE NAPPA

BARBOUR
PUBLISHING, INC.
Uhrichsville, Ohio

The Prayer of Jesus is another creative resource from the authors at Nappaland Communications, Inc. To contact the authors, access their free webzine for families at www.Nappaland.com

Published by Barbour Publishing, Inc., P.O. Box 719, Uhrichsville, Ohio 44683 http://www.barbourbooks.com

Member of the
Evangelical Christian
Publishers Association

Printed in the United States of America.

DEDICATION

For Tom & Jana Tyrrell. You know why.

CONTENTS

For Yours is the kingdom and the power
and the glory forever. Amen!
MATTHEW 6:9–13

INTRODUCTION
IN THIS MANNER,
THEREFORE, PRAY. . .

"Read the words in red. Those are the best parts."

Richard Houle fingered the Bible in his hands. It was an unfamiliar experience, causing a tingle in his soul. Not long ago a friend had shared this advice with him, "If you ever decide to start reading a Bible, read the words in red. Those are the best parts."

And so, holding a red-letter edition of the Scriptures (that is, a Bible that has all the words of Christ printed in red ink), Richard opened the Book—and his heart—to read the messages of God for his life. That experience was a catalyst that changed his life, now and forever. . . .

I'm thinking about my friend Richard today, as I begin the writing of this book you hold in your own hands. That's because I, too, own a "red-letter" edition of the Scriptures, and right now I'm reading the prayer of Jesus in Matthew 6:9–13, marveling at the power of Christ's prayer in this passage.

"In this manner, therefore, pray," He says. "Our Father in heaven, hallowed be Your name. Your kingdom come. Your will be done on earth as it is in heaven. Give us this day our daily bread. And forgive us our debts, as we forgive our debtors. And do not lead us into temptation, but deliver us from the evil one. For Yours is the kingdom and the power and the glory forever. Amen."

Those words spoken so long ago echo through eternity now, waiting to be heard—and lived out—by those of us left behind.

In this manner, therefore, pray. . .

What a gift Jesus Christ has left for us! In a few short sentences, He has shown us what men and women throughout the ages have longed to know: the heart of God for His people's prayers. And we now have the privilege of exploring the Father's heart in the pages of this book. Before we dive into the richness of that exploration, however, I feel that we need clear up something.

There are a few things this prayer of Jesus is *not:*

It's not a legalistic prescription for "proper" prayer. Some would tell you that God only hears us when we speak the exact words of this prayer or other prayers in the Bible.

Friend, that's just not true.

It's not our words that God hears when we

pray; it's our heart. In fact, if you're like me, sometimes you can't even pray with words because your mind refuses to express what you really want to say! Thankfully, God hears—and understands—us no matter what words we speak. The only "proper" prayer is the one where you, a helpless child, call out to God, your all-powerful Father, and there determine to spend time together.

It's not a mantra to be memorized and repeated with mindless arrogance. I've got news for you: God is not impressed by how well you can memorize or how often you can repeat a phrase in prayer. (And if you don't believe me, read Matthew 6:7–8.) He's not spurred to action simply because you remember to quote words to Him on a daily basis.

God *is* interested in what's behind the words we speak. We'd do well to share that same interest in our prayers.

It's not a formula to guarantee that God will always bless you. Every few years, it becomes popular for people to say something like:

"Do this routine, and God will shower blessings upon you!"

"Follow these steps, and God will fill your house with riches of all kinds!"

"Here's the secret to making God bless you!"

Friend, let's be honest. God's primary concern

is not to make sure you're comfortable in this world. Rather, His sole purpose is to help shape you into the image of His one and only Son, Jesus Christ—whatever it takes!

There is no formula for a child to earn his Father's favor. There is only a Father who loves His child enough to bring both good times and bad into life, knowing it takes *both* to accomplish the goal He has set before us.

So what is it then? What is this prayer that Jesus taught us to pray?

It's a model for pursuing intimacy with God, a practical pattern for a lifestyle lived by faith.

What does that mean for you and for me? That, my friend, is what the rest of this little book is all about. So if you are ready—and willing—to explore with me this prayer of Jesus, then turn the page, and let's discover together the power of those "red letters" Christ once spoke for us.

MIKE NAPPA, 2001

1

OUR FATHER

"Hear ye, hear ye," the head angel said. *"The first millennial meeting of the Names of God Committee is now in session. Angel Bubba will lead us in the first order of business."*

A burly angel stood. *"Thank you, Mr. Chairman,"* he said. *"As y'all know, God has recently created a new world, and on the world He's put these things called humans. Now, rumor has it that God's become quite attached to these humans, and He wants a special name for them to use when they talk to God. Our job is to come up with that name."*

"How about His Awesome Majestic Greatness?" suggested one angel.

"Or what about God Triumphant and Powerful?" said another.

"Or, God Who Is Holier Than You'll Ever Be?" said a third angel.

The chairman of the angels scribbled furiously, pleased that there were so many

*lofty names to choose from. Suddenly, the
door to the committee meeting room
burst open, and a messenger angel came
barreling in.*

*"Just got the word from the boss. He's
decided that the humans can call Him
Father."*

*There was an awkward pause, then
pandemonium broke loose in the board
room. "Father!" cried the angels. "But
that's so. . .so personal! It's a family name!
Why would such a powerful God want to
be called that?"*

*The messenger angel shrugged his
shoulders. "Simple," he said. "Because the
humans are His sons and daughters."* [1]

What's in a name? When that name is *Father*,
the answer to that question is *everything*. It's no
mistake that Christ began His prayer in Matthew
6 with these words, "Our *Father*" (italics mine).
With two simple words, Jesus confirmed what
we may already know instinctively: God of all
creation, Master of the universe and everything
beyond, is our Daddy.

Now, if we're honest, the word "father"
doesn't always conjure up positive images in this
sin-soaked society of ours. In fact, we've invented
a whole new vocabulary to describe fathers today:

Deadbeat dads. Alcoholic fathers. Serial abusers. Incestual rapists. Absentee fathers. Family control freaks. Cold. Harsh. Unaffectionate men. Disinterested dads. Workaholic dads. Chauvinist pigs. And the list goes on.

John Trent explains this in terms of a photograph. "We've all grown up with different pictures of what a father is," he says. "Some of the pictures are underexposed: The image is washed out and weak, a passive father maybe, or one without passion. Others are overexposed: The image is dark and frightening, an alcoholic father maybe, or one who is just angry all the time. A few are torn pictures: Only a partial image is left, maybe because the father died or opted for a divorce or just wasn't around to complete the picture. Still others are distorted pictures: The full image is there, but some part of the image is out of balance, too much discipline and too little affection, too much talking and too little listening."[2]

If you want to judge how well a person understands Christianity, find out how much he makes of the thought of being God's child and having God as his Father.

J. I. PACKER

Now here's the good news: Your heavenly Father's not like that. Those faulty pictures may too often be accurate when we're looking at our earthly dads, but we mustn't make the mistake of assuming the poor reflections of fatherhood in our society are reflections of God our Father! God never intended for His name to conjure up associations like that. Our Father isn't like the worst in our earthly fathers; He's the best of those men—and more. He's our life-giver, our caretaker, and the man- and woman-maker we so desperately need to live healthy, fulfilled lives.

OUR FATHER IS A LIFE GIVER

I have a confession to make at this point. Often, my neighbor across the street really annoys me. It's not that Shirley's unkind or noisy or anything like that. In reality, she's a warm, wonderful person and a friend to our entire family.

What annoys me is her yard. Each spring and summer, I gaze out my front window and see. . .*that yard.* Right now as I look across my own lawn I see brown grass and, well, more brown grass. Thirty feet away, in her yard, I see a verdant carpet—lush, thick, and vibrant in color. That's not all. Ringing the yard in glorious splendor is a botanical paradise filled with flowers whose names I can't even pronounce. There are dainty little yellow ones, sprays of purple ones, pink and red ones that reach for the sky, and many others, as well.

What's even worse, I know, is what I can't see from my viewpoint—her backyard. In that place you'll find berry vines and a thriving vegetable garden (from which we often get to eat ourselves!). Shirley's yard is teeming with life, a kind of gardener's paradise. The feeble efforts my wife and I make at simply trying to keep our lawn alive can't even come close to matching the splendor of what Shirley does.

And so it is with God. An earthly father like myself certainly contributes to the beginning of a child's life, but that contribution pales in comparison to the knowledge that our Father God actually *creates* life. Our feeble efforts are merely brown grass next to the garden of God's fathering expertise!

I'm reminded of a story I once read about a physician studying the science of the human body. "The dead body meant nothing at all to me," she reported later. "I could not visualize the man or woman it might have been."

For weeks, this doctor examined cadavers, following with intricate care the mechanisms of human physiology. And slowly a feeling of awe began to engulf her.

"I was working on an arm and hand," she said later, "studying the perfect mechanical arrangements of the muscles and tendons. . . . I was all alone in the laboratory when the overwhelming belief came: a thing like this is not just chance but part of a plan, a plan so big that only God could have conceived it. . . Everything now was evidence of God—the tendons of the hand, the patterns of the little blue butterfly's wings—it was all part of a purpose."[3]

*If you want to see
a picture of the Father,
look at Jesus. . . .
And especially at that
horrible, beautiful
picture Jesus gave us of
blessing others as
He hung on the cross.*

JOHN TRENT

Yes, *that's* our Father. Our Father is the life-giver, the planner of eternity and the moment. When Christ exhorts us to pray "Our Father," He's telling us to revel in the intimacy that comes from knowing personally the author of life!

An interesting thing about our Father: He seems to have made a distinction between "life" and "existence." Look at the world around you. It's not simply an organic machine, plodding daily toward further existence. It's a splashing, ingenious, awe-inspiring sphere that bestows life in colors and shapes and abilities that are beyond our imagination!

This life our Father gives is more than existence. It's Life with a capital "L." Think about it.

God could have created one gray flying animal, but instead he made a toucan, a vulture, an eagle, a mosquito, a butterfly, a bat, and more. He could have made one simple fish, but instead he filled our oceans with whales and dolphins and jellyfish and hammerhead sharks and manta rays and who knows what else that's hidden beneath the depths of the waves. He could have made copies of Adam and Eve, and instead he made you and me and billions upon billions of others of us, each unique and irreplaceable.

The life our Father gives isn't simply a prosaic computer program (existence); it's art (Life!). God intends your life to be painted with joy, with love, with peace, with contentment, and more. By the power of His spirit, your Daddy can fill it (us!) with the textured exuberance of relationships, colors, imagination, hopes and dreams, laughter and tears, joy and tiredness, children smiling, old folks grumbling, and even writers rambling on about things which are, and will always be, unexplainable.

And every inch, every molecule of this Life lies comfortably in the hand of our Father—in the hand that also reaches out to hold your own.

OUR FATHER IS A CARETAKER

"Our Father. . ."

Those words of Christ carry more than just the recognition of God's awesome, life-giving grace toward us. They remind us of the relationship, the family that we have in God.

Like all good fathers, our Father didn't just bring us into this world and then forget about us. How desperate we would be if God had done that! If He'd said, "There, I gave you life. Now you're on your own. Hope you make out okay. See you later!"

No, that's not the kind of Father we have. Our Father is more like Mr. Maurice Rice, the father of John Eades's boyhood friend, Matt. I'll let John Eades explain what he means in his own words here:

> *Mr. Rice was a veteran of World War II, and I remember he was quiet with steel blue eyes and a crew cut. He spoke as if God had put a limit on the number of words he could speak in his lifetime, and he wasn't going to waste even one of them. Since he seldom spoke, I always paid close attention whenever he did, and I noticed the adults did, too. He was definitely a man of few words; and I'm*

positive that in his later years, when he most assuredly went on to heaven, he had a whole bunch of unused words that he turned back in to God.

I remember one night we were playing baseball in another city, and the crowd was plenty rough on us, as if the adults had forgotten we were only eleven years old that summer. There was this huge man standing right behind the backstop, and every time I threw a pitch, he would throw an insult back at me. I saw Mr. Rice come down from the stands and edge right up next to him. In a few seconds the man left the stadium and didn't come back. I didn't know it then, but later I heard my daddy tell my momma that Mr. Rice had simply told the man: "Leave walking or leave stretched out." My daddy voiced his conviction that the abusive man had made a very wise choice.

It sure was comforting to know Mr. Rice was on your side. It gave me a real safe feeling when he was around. When he would treat us to hot dogs after the game, I thought maybe I knew how it felt to be Matt, as Mr. Rice stood there with his smile doing his talking for him. No

*wonder Matt would rather go home after
school than hang around the park with us.
His daddy was really a special man. . . .*

*I can't truly recall the very first time I
got the idea that Mr. Rice might have
had a tendency to lose things, but it seems
it was that time I needed a new pair of
baseball shoes. Being a pitcher, I had
worn out the toe of my right shoe by
pushing off the pitcher's mound and
dragging it across the dirt of the mound
each time I threw a pitch. I'm sure my
momma would have bought me a pair if
she could've, but the truth was we just
didn't have the extra money, especially
since Daddy had begun to make more
frequent stops at the tavern on his way
home from work. I do remember standing beside Mr. Rice's station wagon that
day when he placed his right hand on his
hip pocket as a cloudy, worried look crept
across his usual sunny face.*

*"What's wrong, Mr. Rice?" I asked
him, not believing that such an intelli-
gent man like him could possibly lose his
wallet.*

*"I seem to have lost my billfold," he
answered, checking all of his pockets as he
leaned over and peered into the front seat*

*of the station wagon. "There was a lot of
money in it; I have to find it. I'll go tell
the other boys to start looking for it. I'll
give a twenty-dollar reward to whoever
finds it," he announced as he stared over
toward the ball diamond with me right
behind him like I was a big imprinted
duckling. Suddenly he stopped and
turned around and instructed me to stay
right were I was. "You stay here and
check around on the inside of the station
wagon. Maybe it fell under the seat."*

*I went and opened the driver's door
and bent down, running my hand
beneath the seat as I searched for his wallet. My hand came to rest on his thick
leather billfold, and I clearly recall hit-
ting my head on the doorframe as I raised
up quickly to yell that I had found it.*

*Mr. Rice came back to the car, shook
my hand, and thanked me for the good
deed I had done. He opened his wallet
and pulled out a crisp, new twenty-dollar
bill and handed it to me. "Well, Johnny,"
he said, "what are you going to spend
your reward on?"*

*I glanced down at my white-socked toe
sticking out of my right baseball shoe and
quickly smiled. "I sorta thought I'd get me*

a new pair of baseball shoes, Mr. Rice, but I feel funny about taking the reward money. I didn't do nothing to earn this much." I held the twenty-dollar bill in my hand and pushed it toward him.

Mr. Rice closed my hand over the bill with his hand as he smiled. "You saved me hundreds of dollars, and that's the end of the matter. After practice I'll take you over to Dixie Sporting Goods to be sure you don't spend it on a bunch of foolishness instead of shoes."

That was how Mr. Rice's pattern of losing stuff began. . . . I'm not sure exactly how much stuff he lost when I was growing up, but it seems it was quite a bit as I think back on it. He must have lost his wallet at least a dozen times, and I suppose I became an expert at finding it for him. Of course, he always gave me a reward. . . .

One time I found a brand-new baseball just lying in my front yard on a Sunday morning when Momma and I got home from church. Several times I found a lot of change in the front yard, and most all of the coins were fifty-cent pieces. One time at the Little League field I found a shirt that looked brand-new, *and it was mighty lucky that it happened to be my exact size. One time the mailman brought my momma an anonymous letter addressed to "Youngest Occupant," and it turned out that it contained a free ticket to a Birmingham Barons home game, which luckily Matt and his daddy were going to that very night, so I had a free ride. . . .*

I reckon I could tell you more about Mr. Maurice Rice, but I'm sure you have the picture in focus by now. If ever a natural born loser was born, he was the one, and they broke the mold after him. Sometimes, late at night when it is quiet and everyone is in bed, I think back over my life and realize how selfish I have been in the living of my years. Those nights I get to bed and in the stillness pray to God that He will make me a natural born loser, exactly like Mr. Maurice Rice.[4]

If only we'd all had a "Mr. Rice" in our lives! That caretaker-father example would serve us well when it comes time to trust God's care-full fathering in our own lives. You see, God is more than just our life giver, He—our Father—is also our caretaker through this life and into the life beyond.

An earthly father (hopefully!) commits to care for his child with the best of his resources. He will share food and home, clothing and time, intelligence and sweat, anything he must to care for the young one placed in his care.

Our heavenly Father, too, has made this commitment, and His resources are limitless! He can—and will—use anything and everything to take care of His children. Do you understand what that means? Yes, it means God will provide for your needs, but it also means God has His eyes on all of your needs—physical, emotional, and spiritual. And God will use any means necessary to fulfill His care for you. And sometimes you may not like it!

I remember recently I was digging a trench in my backyard. I rented one of those big, heavy, motorized trenchers and went to work. As I reached one particular area of the yard, up near the house, I always found something blocking me from digging in that spot. A huge rock. A twisted approach. An uncooperative trencher. Finally, after about a half hour of this kind of frustration, I gave up and spent the rest of the day in irritation at my lack of success.

A few days later, an electrician came out to finish by hand the job I'd started with the big machine. "We have a problem," he said, pointing to the area I'd tried in vain to dig up. "I discovered a gas line that runs right along here. We need to move the trench over just a bit."

I stood openmouthed. If God had not frustrated my digging efforts, I surely would have caused the gas line to explode when I cut it forcefully with that mechanized trencher! God, in His fatherly wisdom, was willing to let me get irritated—and saved me from blowing up my house because of it.

Yes, God is our caretaker. Like Mr. Rice, He looks out for us when life's bullies and hardships come. And like He did with my digging endeavor, He also cares enough to let us endure difficulty as part of His loving care over our lives.

OUR FATHER IS A MAN- AND WOMAN-MAKER

Difficulty is sometimes a parent's greatest tool, and our Father isn't shy about making us uncomfortable. Why? Because like all good parents, He's got more in mind than simply feeding and diapering His children. God's desire is for us to *grow,* to get beyond the infancy of faith and become men and women of substance.

Listen to what H. A. Ironside says about this: "Spiritual babies must grow up. Some of the most difficult people to live with in the church of Jesus Christ are those who have grown old in the Lord but haven't grown up in Him. . . May God deliver us from our babyishness!"[5]

An earthly father would be no loving parent to insist his seventeen-year-old child remain in diapers, sleep in a crib, and digest strained peas and milk for sustenance. We'd consider that to be criminal! A father's responsibility is to care for his child and through that caring to help that child learn skills and attitudes to survive success-fully as an adult. Each year my wife and I add to the responsibilities and chores our son must do. We're not trying to get a free ride or treat him like a slave (which is sometimes what he thinks!). Instead, we're training him to take care of himself so that eventually he'll be able to care for himself.

Likewise, our heavenly Father would be no loving parent to allow us to remain in the safety of a spiritual "nursery" for our time on this earth. Since God truly loves us, He sends us out into that great, uncomfortable, often difficult world in which we live. To do less than that would be to stunt our natural ability to grow in grace and in the likeness of His Son, Jesus Christ.

Consider the example of the shark. I'm told that the normal length of a healthy, full-grown shark is about eight feet. An interesting thing about the shark, though, is the way it grows. Surely you've been to large aquariums and seen sharks much smaller than eight feet—even some as small as your hand. The reason is that sharks tend to grow in a size proportionate to their surroundings. That means if you catch a small shark and place it in a small aquarium, the shark will grow to a limit that fits within that space. In fact, a full-grown shark can actually be as small as six inches or so, depending on where it lives![6]

The refusal to look up to God as our Father is the one central wrong in the whole human affair.

GEORGE MACDONALD

An anonymous writer in *Leadership* magazine once made this comment about that phenomenon: "That also happens to some Christians. I've seen some of the cutest little six-inch Christians who swim around in a little puddle. But if you put them into a larger arena—into the whole creation—only then can they become great."[7]

Here's where we have it better than the shark. We never have to go out into the big, bad world all alone. God, our Father, our life giver, our caretaker, is constantly at our side, guiding, protecting, cheering us on to grow and mature into the people He envisions us to be. Sure, He will place us in uncomfortable situations along the way, but He always stands nearby, ready to assist and direct us as we grow from boys and girls into His men and women.

John Trent remembers a time when his mother helped him learn to become a man in a similar way. "I remember when [my twin brother] Jeff and I turned ten, [my mother] dressed us up in our finest sports coats and clip-on ties." John's mother then took them all out to a fancy restaurant for a birthday dinner. During dinner, she explained that her boys were now "young men," and that she expected them to begin acting like men in social situations. At the end of the meal, much to the boys' surprise, she passed them each a dollar and told them they were to leave it as a tip.

John says, "It was a rite-of-passage for us, for from that day on we were expected to take more and more responsibility. My mother never paid another bill when we were with her. She would slide us money under the table, and we would assume that duty. We were learning, through her soft hands and gentle proddings to become gentlemen. We were beginning to grow up."[8]

Take joy in the fact that God is your Father. Delight in the fact that He daily gives you life, and that He's committed to caring for you each moment of each day. And most of all, thank Him for not letting you live your life in spiritual diapers. When you feel His discipline, when you find He's thrust you into some uncomfortable situation that seems more than you're ready for, when you feel Him pushing you to exercise your spiritual muscles of prayer, worship, Scripture study, and more—rejoice! It means your Father cares enough to help you grow out of childhood and into a man or woman that He will be proud of from here to eternity.

After all, Jesus has made it clear. This God we speak of is also. . .

"Our Father!"

FOR FURTHER REFLECTION. . .

Since you are God's children, God sent the Spirit of his Son into your hearts, and the Spirit cries out, "Father." So now you are not a slave; you are God's child, and God will give you the blessing he promised, because you are his child.

GALATIANS 4:6–7 NCV

"Which of you, if his son asks for bread, will give him a stone? Or if he asks for a fish, will give him a snake? If you, then, though you are evil, know how to give good gifts to your children, how much more will your Father in heaven give good gifts to those who ask him!"

MATTHEW 7:9–10 NIV

So you should not be like cowering, fearful slaves. You should behave instead like God's very own children, adopted into his family—calling him "Father, dear Father." For his Holy Spirit speaks to us deep in our hearts and tells us that we are God's children.

ROMANS 8:15–16 NLT

2

IN HEAVEN

"Our Father in heaven. . ."

Christ seemed to pray these words so casually, and my temptation today is to skip over them to dig into the rest of the prayer of Jesus. Yet doing so would rob us of the implicit promise wrapped up in one awe-inspiring word:

Heaven.

I don't know about you, but sometimes I get so homesick for heaven that it hurts. I feel the longing for God's glorious paradise like a dog left at home all day while the master is off at work or on a trip. I perk my ears at every sound, waiting, hoping that soon I'll hear my master's voice calling me out to play.

Heaven.

I'm struck by the fact that God didn't have to create a place for me to spend eternity with Him. Truthfully, He could have arranged it so that death was simply the end, and that would have been enough. But that's not what our Father intended for His children, is it? Apparently, God likes happy endings, and He's written one for each and every one of us adopted into His family.

Listen to what Jesus promised:

"There are many rooms in my Father's home, and I am going to prepare a place for you. If this were not so, I would tell you plainly. When everything is ready, I will come and get you, so that you will always be with me where I am" (John 14:2–3 NLT).

Heaven.

Despite all that we deserve, Jesus Himself is preparing eternity for us and making plans to usher us personally into His paradise.

For some, that truth may seem an uncomfortable one. I'm reminded of the story of a young boy attending a new Sunday school class. The teacher expounded long and hard about pearly gates and streets of gold, ending her little talk with an invitation.

"How many of you here want to go to heaven?" she asked enthusiastically.

All members of the class quickly raised their hands—except one. The new boy simply looked grim-faced and didn't move. So the teacher talked a moment more about the great joys that await us in heaven, then issued her call again.

"Now, how many of you would like to go to heaven?"

Again, all hands went up, save the boy's. This time he actually sat on his hands in defiance. The teacher was heartbroken. "Young man," she said sympathetically, "why don't you want to go to heaven when you die?"

A look of blissful relief crossed the boy's face, and he freed his hands. "Oh," he said. "Yes, I do want to go to heaven when I die. It's just that I thought you were getting together a carload to leave for heaven right now!"

Heaven goes by favor.
If it went by merit,
you would stay out,
and your dog would go in.

MARK TWAIN

HEAVEN IS LIKE. . .

We may chuckle at this story, but it also reveals the hidden uncertainty we often carry in regard to heaven. What if heaven isn't all it's cracked up to be? I mean, we'll be there forever, right? What if we get bored or tired or something like that?

Larry Libby, in his book *Someday Heaven*, asked a similar question. In response, he imagined himself as a little bird living each day in a tiny, rusted cage. After a time, a kind person takes that bird and frees it in a mighty forest. This forest is filled with glorious sunlight, gushing waterfalls, flowering trees and plants, and millions of other birds all singing, playing, and eating their fill throughout the beautiful flora and fauna of the forest.

"Now, little bird," Libby says, "can you imagine wanting to stay in your cage? Can you imagine saying, 'Oh please don't let me go. I will miss my cage. I will miss my little food dish with seeds in it. I will miss my plastic mirror and my tiny little perch. I might get bored in that big forest.'

"That would be silly wouldn't it? And it's just as silly to think we might run out of things to do in heaven!"[1]

I love this picture Libby paints of heaven as a life-giving forest of wonder and joy, but I still find myself asking, "What will heaven be like, really?"

Mary and Bill Barbour asked several children in Newton Square, Pennsylvania, that question, and got many wonderful answers![2]

"I think heaven will be glamorous," said eight-year-old Becca, "shining, sparkling, glorious, and wonderful. . . . I think there will be angels, and Daniel will be there, and Mary, Joseph, Rebekah, and Rahab. I think it will be amazing. Heaven will be the best place ever."

Nine-year-old Abigail described it this way: "I think heaven will be made with gold and will be prettier than the nicest things ever. And heaven will be perfect. You'll have everything you want."

"I think heaven is going to be very fun," said nine-year-old Michael. "I wonder if we could swim in water and not get wet. That would be fun if we could walk through flowers. And be really good in math."

And I love what nine-year-old Heather had to say about it: "I think that heaven will be beautiful, and it'll be bright from God. Maybe the streets of gold will be so bright that we'll have to wear sunglasses!"

Truth is, there's no way our finite minds can ever comprehend the infinite beauty and peace and joy that God is preparing for us. But that shouldn't stop us from being like those children in Pennsylvania and trying to imagine it! Notable authors Bruce & Stan agree, saying:

> *There is no image more worthy of your imagination than heaven. We all think about heaven from time to time—we can't help it (Eccles. 3:11)—but too often we limit our imagination to "streets of gold" (Rev. 21:21) and "mansions" (John 14:2 KJV). It's okay to think about heaven the way you would think about Disneyland, with castles, fantasy lands, and thrill rides. But don't limit your thoughts to the happiest place on Earth. Heaven will be much more than we have*

ever seen or could imagine (1 Cor. 2:9).

When you fill your mind with the infinite possibilities of heaven, you have no choice but to think about God. . . .

One big dream every Christian should have centers on the stuff God has prepared for us beyond this life on Earth (1 Cor. 2:9). This is not a fantasy land (although the mansions and gold streets may seem like that). Heaven is for real. When you dream of heaven, you are dreaming of something very realistic. This should give you tremendous motivation to serve God on Earth and love Him with your whole being. . . . Heaven isn't something from a fairy tale. It's a very real place that Jesus is preparing for those who have put their faith in Him. It is a place that will have no tears, pain, sorrow, or death. It is the hope of all who believe in Christ." [3]

So what do you dream that heaven is like? I imagine that. . .

heaven is like a football game, with cheers and
    excitement and adrenaline-rushing events;
heaven is like a silence that crackles through a
    crisp winter night, bringing with it a tin-
    gling freshness in every breath;

heaven is like a party with friends who laugh
and play games and tell stories about these,
the good old days;
heaven is like a Sunday afternoon feast with
only the good stuff (pizza and chocolate
and such) served up on the table;
heaven is like a tension-draining embrace from
my wife, when the simple touch of her
hand soothes the pain in my head and
relaxes my body into a welcome, dreamless
sleep;
and perhaps best of all, heaven is finally the
one place I can truly call home.

HEAVEN IS YOUR HOME—
AND THE DOOR IS ALWAYS OPEN

"The first time I traveled with my mother and
sister to my parents' homeland of Tonadico di
Primero in Northern Italy, I felt I'd been there
before," says Joseph Cardinal Bernadin.

How was this possible, since Bernadin had
never been to this place before? Was it some
kind of weird déjà vu or a clue to a secret past?

No, nothing so mysterious. Bernardin explains, "After years of looking through my
mother's photo albums, I knew the mountains,
the land, the houses, the people. As soon as we

entered the valley, I said, 'I know this place. I am home.' Somehow I think crossing from this life into life eternal will be similar. I will be home."[4]

What a beautiful way of describing the home-coming that awaits the children of our Father! Day after day, we are given the opportunity to see "pictures of heaven" in the Bible, in our churches, in the lives of other Christians, and yes, in the way our spirits interact with God's Spirit. And with each little encounter, we gain a slightly clearer image of heaven, our true home.

I went home recently, to the streets of an Oklahoma City suburb where I grew up. I have to admit, it wasn't the sweet, nostalgic experience we often associate with home. Oh, sure, I spent time with relatives and enjoyed their company very much. But the place just wasn't the same. It was smaller, for one thing. The place that had once been my world, my "stomping grounds," so to speak, was now simply a few exits on a busy freeway. It was crowded—traffic spilled out everywhere—and it was dirty and run-down in places. The people were rude or indifferent, and I found myself not caring that my old neigh-borhood was deteriorating by degrees.

As I drove away, I realized why this home-coming of mine left something to be desired. It was because I wasn't home. Sure, I had gone to a place where I'd once lived, but simply living there didn't make it my home. My true home is located in a place I can't see. And it has all the best of the places I've lived—family, friends, memories, laughter—and none of the worst. No gangs, no taxes, no poverty, no angry words or violent acts. My true home is heaven! Everything my earthly homes lack awaits for me there—and more I can't even imagine!

Here's something I adore about my heavenly home: The door is always open, and the furniture is hands-on!

I remember once, during my freshman year in college, I decided to surprise my mother by driving home unannounced for a holiday weekend. My roommate and I drove through the night, and around 6:00 A.M. on Saturday morning, we pulled into my driveway.

Won't Mom be surprised to see me? I thought as I grabbed my duffel bag and walked up to the front porch. Fitting my key into the lock, I discovered a big surprise. It didn't work. I tried it again and again before the reality set in that my mother had changed the locks in my absence! Then I peeked in the front window and discovered someone else's furniture in my living room. It was my turn to be surprised, because it appeared that my dear sweet mother had moved away while I was gone—and forgotten to tell me about it!

Actually, she'd just gone on a weekend retreat

with her church. Since her roommate had moved out recently (taking the living room furniture with her), my mother had bought a new couch and chair and had gone ahead and changed the locks as a safety precaution. And, yes, I did eventually get back into my house, but I've never forgotten that feeling when I stood on the porch locked out of my own home!

Isn't it great to know that we never have to experience that feeling about heaven? Thanks to Jesus Christ and His sacrificial work on the cross, the door to heaven will never be closed to us! He stands at the opening Himself, beckoning us inside to meet the Father and enjoy our time in this, our true home.

There have been times when I think we do not desire heaven, but more often I find myself wondering whether, in our heart of hearts, we have ever desired anything else.

C. S. LEWIS

Which brings to mind another image for me. I remember as a child a time when my grandfather gave my grandmother a gift of an all-new, fancy living room set of furniture. Finest quality, stylish design. The best she'd ever owned.

In fact, it was so nice that (for a time) she forbade us grandchildren from sitting on it unless it had a plastic covering on it! The idea of eating a snack on the couch was unthinkable. This stuff was so precious that it made me feel like an unwelcome guest in my grandmother's house. (If you've ever met my grandmother, you know it's nearly impossible for anyone to feel unwelcome there!) Eventually my Nanaw got over the newness of that furniture, and we kids reclaimed her house as our own, but for that short time it had been a "hands-off" environment.

Not so with heaven! This place that God is preparing for us is so "hands-on" that I'm told God will give us brand-new bodies to go along with it![5] Heaven's parlor won't be a place where we must tread lightly and solemnly. It'll be a playroom of sorts where we will dance and laugh and sing and cartwheel over tables if we want. And the best part of this hands-on heaven is that we ourselves will be able to reach out and touch the face of God in that place.

DON'T WAIT UNTIL YOU'RE DEAD TO EXPERIENCE HEAVEN!

I heard a story once about a poor young couple sitting in a church service where the pastor was preaching about heaven. "It's a place where there's no such thing as money," the preacher said.

Quickly checking his empty wallet, the young husband leaned over and squeezed his wife. "Well," the young man whispered, "we must be in heaven already!"

If lack of finances were the measure of heaven, then I, too, have been there many times already! But the truth is, heaven is not so far away from any of us. You see, although it's true that God resides in heaven, it's also true that heaven resides wherever God is. That's so important, I'm going to repeat it for you:

Heaven resides wherever God is.

Think about it. Heaven's real attraction isn't streets of gold or walls of jasper or absence of pain and tears or even the fact that our loved ones will inhabit that place. Sure, those things are wonderful, but what makes heaven *heaven* isn't that dear Aunt Susie is there.

It's that *our Father* is there.

Remove God from heaven and it's no longer heaven. It's just a nice, eternally incomplete place. For that reason, we can be grateful that heaven itself is the place where we encounter the awesome, majestic, incomprehensible God![16]

Do you see what that means for you and me? God isn't captured and secluded in some unreachable celestial spot. No, *heaven is wherever God is*—and that means your life need never be the same again.

Anyplace where God is, heaven can also be. That means if God is in your life, in your heart, in your soul, in your spirit, in your attitudes, in your work, in your home, in your relationships, in your very being, then traces of heaven can be found in each of those places as well. You can literally experience heaven on earth; why wait until you die? It's all a matter of perspective and of recognizing that heaven can fill the moments all around you today.

I like the way theologian Ron Rhodes expounds on this concept. He says:

> *The incredible glory of the afterlife— our real life—should motivate each of us to live faithfully during our relatively short time on earth. Especially when difficult times come, we must remember that we are only pilgrims on our way to anther land—to the undiscovered country, the final frontier of heaven where God Himself dwells.*
>
> *J. I. Packer once said that the "lack of long, strong thinking about our promised hope of glory is a major cause of our plodding, lackluster lifestyle." Packer points to the Puritans as a much-needed example for us, for they believed that "it is the heavenly Christian that is the lively Christian."*

I am particularly impressed with the writings of the Puritan Richard Baxter. Truly he had some habits worthy of imitation. His first habit was to "estimate everything—values, priorities, possessions, relationships, claims, tasks—as these things will appear when one actually comes to die." In other words, he weighed everything in terms of eternal benefit. After all, our life on earth is short; our life in heaven is forever. If we work only for the things of this earth, what eternal benefit will all of it have?

Baxter's second habit was to "dwell on the glory of the heavenly life to which one was going." Baxter daily practiced "holding heaven at the forefront of his thoughts and desires." The hope of heaven brought him joy, and joy brought him strength. Baxter once said, "A heavenly mind is a joyful mind; this is the nearest and truest way to live a life of comfort.... A heart in heaven will be a most excellent preservative against temptations, a powerful means to kill thy corruptions."

Christian apologists Gary R. Habermas and J. P. Moreland have come up with a term I like a lot: a "top-down" perspective. That's precisely what we need

during our earthly pilgrimage as we jour-
ney toward our heavenly destiny:

The God of the universe invites us to
view life and death from His eternal
vantage point. And if we do, we will see
how readily it can revolutionize our lives:
daily anxieties, emotional hurts,
tragedies, our responses and responsibili-
ties to others, possessions, wealth, and
even physical pain and death. All of this
and much more can be informed and
influenced by the truths of heaven. The
repeated witness of the New Testament is
that believers should view all problems,
indeed, their entire existence, from what
we call the "top-down" perspective: God
and His kingdom first, followed by vari-
ous aspects of our earthly existence. . . .
Our goal, then, should be to maintain a
"top-down" perspective. This perspective is
a radical love of God that places Him
first and foremost in every aspect of our
lives. "Set your mind on things above, not
on earthly things" (Colossians 3:2 [NIV]).
And when we do this, God has promised
to meet all our earthly needs as part of
the package (Matthew 6:33)! [7]

Do you need a little heaven in your life

today? Then perhaps it's time you sought out the author of heaven. Perhaps it's time we all determined to live life from a "top-down" perspective; to immerse ourselves in intimacy with the Father who has created heaven for us. When we do that, we literally bring a life-changing taste of heaven down here to earth.

Now, I'd be remiss if I ended this chapter with the assumption that you've already begun this intimate relationship with God. I hope you have, because I so want to discover you in heaven! But I want to spell this out plainly for you, and I don't want you to think I've deliberately hidden truth from you. If you've not yet committed your life to Christ, let me tell you here how you can meet God and begin this relationship with the Creator of heaven.

First, you must understand that you and I have failed. From day one to this, we have fallen short of God's expectations for our lives. The Bible calls that "sin," and is very clear in saying "For all have sinned; all fall short of God's glorious standard" (Romans 3:23 NLT).

That poses a problem, because sin, like a deadly virus, brings spiritual death to us. For the answer, God sent His one and only Son, Jesus Christ, to live on earth as a man. Here He bore the penalty of our sin through His execution on the cross. But He didn't stop there.

On the third day after His execution, He proved His power over life and death and sin by returning to life once more. He is still alive even today, and now offers spiritual life to all who would believe in Him and trust their lives to His care.

Listen to what the Bible says about it:

"The wages of sin is death, but the free gift of God is eternal life through Christ Jesus our Lord" (Romans 6:23 NLT).

"For if you confess with your mouth that Jesus is Lord and believe in your heart that God raised him from the dead, you will be saved. For it is by believing in your heart that you are made right with God, and it is by confessing with your mouth that you are saved. As the Scriptures tell us, 'Anyone who believes in him will not be disappointed' " (Romans 10:9–11 NLT).

And so you now have a choice. Will you begin that life with Jesus? Accept His offer of forgiveness for sin and eternal life? Trust your every action and very being to His care and leading?

If your answer is yes, you can meet Him right now. Lay down this book and pray. Admit to Jesus what He already knows—that you have sinned and need His forgiveness. Tell Him you want to receive His offer of eternal life. Ask Him to help you live out His desires for you from this day forward and to help you grow moment by moment in intimacy with Him.

When your prayer is finished, call someone and tell him or her what you've just done! A Christian friend or family member, perhaps, or the pastor at a local Christian church. Ask them to help you learn more about how to grow in your new relationship with Jesus.

Go ahead and put the book down now to do that. I'll meet you again in the next chapter—and then, one glorious day, in heaven.

FOR FURTHER REFLECTION. . .

"There are many rooms in my Father's home, and I am going to prepare a place for you."

JOHN 14:2 NLT

Then I saw a new heaven and a new earth, for the first heaven and the first earth had passed away, and there was no longer any sea. I saw the Holy City, the new Jerusalem, coming down out of heaven from God, prepared as a bride beautifully dressed for her husband. And I heard a loud voice from the throne saying, "Now the dwelling of God is with men, and he will live with them. They will be his people, and God himself will be with them and be their God. He will wipe every tear from their eyes. There will be no more death or mourning or crying or pain, for the old order of things has passed away."

REVELATION 21:1–4 NIV

For God has not destined us for wrath, but for obtaining salvation through our Lord Jesus Christ, who died for us, so that whether we are awake or asleep, we will live together with Him. Therefore encourage one another and build up one another, just as you also are doing.

1 THESSALONIANS 5:9–11 NASB

3

HALLOWED
BE YOUR NAME

Perhaps you've heard of Joseph "Fighting Joe"
Hooker. A career soldier, he was an American
hero during the Civil War. He was wounded at
the Battle of Antietam in 1862, yet managed to
recover well enough to continue fighting and
even to achieve the rank of brigadier general. At
one point (by order of Abraham Lincoln himself) Joe was given charge of the Union's main
fighting force, the Army of the Potomac, and en-
trusted with winning the war for the North.

He was a decorated soldier as well, and received a prestigious "Thanks of Congress" award
for his stellar defense of Baltimore and Washington D.C. Only fifteen generals in all of the Civil
War received this congressional designation!

Even if you don't know of Fighting Joe,
chances are you know his name. You see, this
American hero was recognized for more than
just his fighting prowess. Whenever his army
encamped at a new location, Joe was known for
rounding up local prostitutes to "serve" his men
and "improve morale."

Charles Francis Adams Jr. (grandson of president John Quincy Adams and great-grandson of president John Adams) described Joe's headquarters this way, "A place where no self-respecting man liked to go and no decent woman could go. It was a combination of barroom and brothel."

Joe's reputation reached the streets of Washington D.C. itself. When a "red-light" district of sorts arose in a seedier side of the capital city, the locals there quickly branded it with the general's name. Civil War historian, Bruce Catton, reveals, "During these war years, Washington developed a large [red-light district] somewhere south of Constitution Avenue. This became known as Hooker's Division in tribute to the proclivities of General Joseph Hooker and the name has stuck ever since."

It wasn't long before that designation was shortened to "Hooker's," then simplified to "hookers" and used as slang references to prostitutes nationwide. Now, more than a century later, few Americans can tell you that Joseph Hooker was a war hero. Millions, however, still recognize his name—as just another synonym for a sex peddler.[1]

You see where I'm going with this, don't you? Joseph Hooker had the potential for his name to be remembered with high honor;

instead, his lifestyle ensured that his name is remembered in disgrace.

And that brings me to the next portion of the prayer of Jesus—the part about the name.

"Our Father in heaven," Jesus prays, "Hallowed be Your name. . ."

Take notice, now. This is the first "request" of this prayer of Jesus! It speaks volumes that Christ didn't dive into a litany of personal needs at this point. After acknowledging His Father in heaven, Christ's first—and some might argue His foremost—desire in prayer is for God's name to be regarded in holy ("hallowed") reverence.

The New Living Translation of the Scripture interprets this phrase in contemporary, reader-friendly terms: "may your name be honored." Either way, the intent behind the words is still the same:

God's name is *important.*

It's important to the Father, it's important to the Son (Jesus), and it needs to be important to us. When we, like Christ, pray the words "Hallowed be Your name," or

By the name of God, I understand a Substance infinite (eternal, immutable), independent, all knowing, all powerful, and by which I myself, and every other thing that exists. . .were created.

RENÉ DESCARTES

"May Your name be honored," we do more than simply say a few nice words. We make ourselves partners in the desire to bring honor and respect and holy reverence to God and His reputation.

So how exactly do we "hallow" or "honor" God's name? It happens in three ways: in the way we worship, in the way we live, and in the way we love.

WE HONOR GOD'S NAME
BY THE WAY WE WORSHIP

In case you weren't aware of it, the term that we translate as "God" in English versions of the Bible is actually a conglomeration of many names the original writers used to designate Him. Each of these names for God are important because they represent the personality and power of our limitless creator in ways our limited intellects can comprehend—at least a little.

When we begin to understand the truth that these names reveal about God, we've taken the first step toward honoring God's name by the way we worship. After all, what is worship anyway but us recognizing the truth about God and His unbounded greatness?

This is critical for us to understand. God isn't some insecure egotist who needs us to keep telling Him how great He is in order to feel good about Himself. We are the ones in need—in need of seeing the truth about ourselves, our world, and about God. When we recognize that truth, the natural result is worship—a personal, intimate "honoring" of God by admitting the truth; and that's an experience that can literally revolutionize your life!

What do these ancient names reveal about God? What truths do they lay clear for us to praise about Him? Entire books have been written on that subject! But let me share with you a few of my favorites from the names of God used in the Bible.[2]

Yahweh

Sometimes called the "proper name" of God, Yahweh is generally regarded as the most holy designation for our creator. According to theologian Ken Hemphill, it carries with it "the idea of life itself. . . The name implies that God is absolutely self-existent. He is the One who in Himself possesses life and permanent existence. He alone!" It's this name that forms the root for the English phrase "I AM" recorded in Exodus 3, where God tells Moses to tell the Israelites that "I AM" sent him to deliver the people from slavery. And so when we worship Yahweh, we give adoration to the great I AM, to the eternal source of life and existence!

An interesting side note here: In Hebrew, this name is written without vowels as "YHWH." Ancient Israelites considered this name so holy that they wouldn't even pronounce it out loud for fear of debasing the name! In the German language, YHWH was translated as "JHVH"— and that eventually was broadened to the name "Jehovah" which we can often find in English translations of the Bible.

El Shaddai

Made popular several years ago thanks to a song by Amy Grant, El Shaddai is beautiful in both its simplicity and its meaning: God Almighty! That about sums it up, doesn't it? He is God, and He is almighty! Nothing is beyond His ability; no one can truly oppose Him; never will weakness command Him. He (your Father!) is El Shaddai, God Almighty. Thus, when we want to worship God's limitless power and ability, we can raise our hands and declare, "El Shaddai!"

Jehovah Jireh

Here God begins to reveal the tender Fatherhood that so characterizes the way He relates to you and me. Why? Because this name of God is more than descriptive in meaning—it carries a promise. Jehovah Jireh, coined by the patriarch

Abraham, means "the Lord will provide." Abraham "named" God this after the Lord provided a sacrifice to use in place of Abraham's son Isaac. Today the name is still a reminder of God's awesome power to provide for us. . .but that's a subject for a later chapter (chapter 6, to be exact). And so, when we feel ourselves overflowing with praise for God's gracious provisions in our lives, we can worship and honor Him by calling out His name, "Jehovah Jireh."

Other names for God that can prompt us to worship our incredible Father include: *Jehovah Rohi* (God our shepherd); *Jehovah Shammi* (the Lord who is there); *Jehovah Rophi* (God who heals); and *El Elyon* (God most high)!

"Hallowed be Your name," Jesus prayed for us—and what a name that is! It encompasses all these names we've discussed—and more. Simply recognizing these names humbles me; this great God of all allows me (and you) to take part in the honoring of His awesome name! May His name be honored in the truth of our worship.

As Hemphill points out, "Understanding the names of God will help us to understand how to praise and worship Him more effectively. . . . His name is great, and He is worthy of our praise. Like an earthly father, He must rejoice when He hears his children praise Him with the use of His name."

WE HONOR GOD'S NAME
BY THE WAY WE LIVE

Our first priority then is to honor God's name in praise and worship, in recognizing the truth of His eternal greatness. Yet hallowing God's name doesn't stop there, because we also honor God by the way we live (which itself is an act of worship as well.)

In Ken Hemphill's excellent book, *The Names of God,* he shares a story about the day he left home to become a freshman student at Wake Forest University. After saying his good-byes to his mother in the house, Ken's father walked him out to the car for a few last words. The young man expected a little lecture that listed dos and don'ts Dad wanted him to follow while away at school.

> *I want people to look at me and say, "What a great God we serve," not "What a great guy!"*
>
> NBA CHAMPION,
> DAVID ROBINSON

Instead, the father said, "Son, I've only got one thing of value to give you, and that's my name. Don't take my name anywhere I wouldn't take it, and don't do anything with my name that I wouldn't do with it. That's my only request as you go off to college."

Want to guess what happened after that? That's right. From that day forward, Ken Hemphill measured his every action by his father's charge. If he deemed going to a certain activity would reflect poorly on the family name, he didn't go. In his classes and social activities, he carried himself in such a way as to bring honor—not dishonor—to the name his father had given him. And at the time of this writing, Ken Hemphill has done his father proud, living a lifetime of faith in Christ and even acting as president of a prominent theological seminary.

Like Papa Hemphill, our heavenly Father has passed His good name on to us. The question, then, is how are we adding to the family reputation?

I remember watching a newscast in recent years covering the scandal then-president Bill Clinton went through over his affair with a young White House intern, Monica Lewinsky. The word "Lewinsky" began to be used for a particular intimate act. After watching the practice spread from publication to publication, Monica Lewinsky's father finally had to issue a press statement, begging writers to discontinue using his name to mean that act!

I was impressed by the elder Lewinsky's action but dismayed that his daughter had thought so little of the name he'd passed on to her. I would like to say that we Christians have done a much better job than Monica Lewinsky at protecting the name of our Father's family, but sadly, we're often guilty of adding unwanted associations to God's name as well.

We have taken God's holy name and, through our attitudes and actions, added unattractive—and untrue—adjectives to it. Here are a few that I've heard us called of late:

Hateful. Bigoted. Intolerant. Insipid. Dishonest. Overbearing. Unkind. Disrespectful. Murderous. Arrogant. Power-hungry. Money-grubbing. Unethical. Antieverything. Out of touch. Dangerous. Criminal. Weak-willed. Abusive. Conniving. Violent. Insane. Heartless. Easily deceived. Contentious. And the list goes on.

God never intended His family name to be known by these terms. Sadly, too many of these adjectives are true today—and have been true for some time. This is not to say that we should adopt a namby-pamby, anything-goes-as-long-as-we-look-good style of faith. That kind of shallow reputation isn't what God desires, either. But it is to say that we've done a poor job of carrying God's family name with honor.

Here's why: We've forgotten that the greatest honor we can give to God's name is to be known by the actions of Jesus Christ. That is, to be known as a servant of the first, best servant who gave His life as a ransom for ours.

God doesn't call us to be kings or presidents or politicians or celebrities or members of high society (though He may indeed place us in those kinds of positions). What God calls us most to be is *servants;* people who serve Him by serving others. In that role alone are we best enabled to honor our Lord's name.

Who adds to God's reputation best, the hate-filled preacher who rails against abortion doctors and carries placards that shout "Murderer!" in front of clinic doors? Or the woman who befriends a teenage mother and helps her learn the skills needed for positive parenting?

Who brings more glory to God's name, the boycotting organizations that refuse to watch television because the network gives health insurance benefits to its homosexual employees? Or the man who volunteers in an AIDS hospice to help ease the suffering of homosexual people stricken with this horrible disease?

I think we can learn much from the example of Catherine Lawes.[3] When her husband became warden of Sing Sing Prison in 1921, friends and relatives alike warned her not to step foot into the prison. At that time, Sing Sing was known for housing the worst of the worst, criminals most assumed were beyond rehabilitation. Catherine was a young woman and mother of three small children; certainly this prison was no place for her!

But Catherine also belonged to another family—the family of God. As a result, she didn't view those held in Sing Sing as anything less than they were: men. "My husband and I are going to take care of these men," she announced, and then proceeded to pour her life into serving the "worst of the worst."

When the basketball game was to be played in the prison, Catherine Lawes gathered her children and sat in the stands among the inmates, cheering and clapping for the players. When she discovered one convicted murderer was blind, she spent countless hours with him, personally teaching the man how to read Braille. Another time she met a deaf-mute person in the cells of Sing Sing. Moved to serve him, she went to school to learn how to use sign language so she could communicate with that prisoner—and help him to communicate with others.

Mrs. Lawes served these prisoners of Sing Sing until her untimely death in 1937. At her funeral, hardened criminals wept openly at losing this woman who had been their servant—and their friend. Later, the warden's wife received the greatest compliment anyone could ever receive.

"Catherine Lawes," it was said, "was the body of Jesus that came alive again in Sing Sing Prison from 1921 to 1937."

So how can we honor God's great name? The same way Catherine Lawes did, by living a lifestyle of service and grace. And by a rugged determination to love others like our Father has loved us.

WE HONOR GOD'S NAME BY THE WAY WE LOVE

Let's get something straight at this point. We need not serve God out of mere obligation or a sense of duty. We serve and honor His name out of passion, out of deep love for God.

Love is the fuel; service, simply the movement generated by our passion for God and His Word. This kind of loving service reflects the love of the Father and thus brings honor to the family name He has given us to share. In short, we honor God's name in the way we love God and the people He created.

I'm reminded of the true story of a teenager in the former Soviet Union during the 1970s.[4] Under strict Communist rule, it was illegal to practice the Christian faith in that country at that time, and Bibles were a scarce commodity. In spite of that, millions of people still participated in "underground" church services and Bible studies.

At one such Bible study, a teenage girl joined a small group of Christians gathered in a home to read and examine the Scriptures. As the pastor of the group was reading a verse, suddenly the door burst open, and Communist soldiers flooded the room, guns in hand. The soldiers insulted and terrorized the Christians, threatening prison and worse for having broken the law with their illegal meeting.

After a time, the ranking officer pointed his gun at the pastor's head and demanded the Bible the group had been using. Reluctantly, the pastor gave the Book to the soldier.

The Communist threw the Bible to the floor in scorn. Then he turned to the fearful Christians and snarled, "We will let you go. But first you must spit on this book of lies. Anyone who refuses will be shot."

"You first," a fellow soldier commanded, motioning with his gun at a man in the congregation. With painful slowness, the man knelt by the Bible lying at the leading soldier's feet. "Father, please forgive me," he whispered, then he spit on the book. He stood, and the soldiers parted from the doorway, allowing him to leave.

The soldiers motioned for another person, a woman, to do the act of scorn. Tears in her eyes, she also spit on the Bible and was then allowed to leave.

At that point the teenage girl stepped forward. Reportedly "overcome with love for her Lord," this teen stooped down and picked up the Bible. Ignoring the flush of anger rising within the soldier next to her, she whispered a prayer.

"What have they done to Your Word? Please forgive them." And, using her own dress, she carefully wiped the spit off the cover of God's Word. That act of love was her last in this world, as she was murdered by the head soldier moments later.

Do you have that kind of love for God? A love that moves you to willingly sacrifice your life in honor of His name? I'm not sure that I do, either—yet. But you and I can still be encouraged by the example of love displayed decades ago in the heart and actions of this nameless teenage girl. By God's grace, we, too, can be so overcome with love for our Father that our every action will bring honor to His name.

Loving God doesn't stop there, though. Yes, we allow God's name to be holy and honored through our passionate love for Him. But we do the same through our love for His children as well.

Christ once declared, "Your love for one another will prove to the world that you are my disciples" (John 13:35 NLT). What a great thing to be known for! As part of the Father's family, as children who carry His name, we get the privilege of being known by the way we love others!

Think about it. The Rockefeller family is known for its wealth. The Turner family is known for its media offerings. The Kennedy and Bush families are known for their political involvements.

> *In the name of God:*
> *respect, protect,*
> *love and serve life,*
> *every human life! . . .*
> *We must love others with*
> *the same love which*
> *God pours into our hearts.*
>
> POPE JOHN PAUL II

You and I? We get to be known for our love! Can you think of anything better to be known for? Me neither.

What is our example of love to follow then? The Father Himself. In the parable of the prodigal son, Christ revealed much about how our Father loves—and how we can love as well.

It seems a certain wealthy man had a son who was impatient to get his family riches. So the boy went to his father and demanded his inheritance, even though the old man wasn't dead yet. The father granted the son his wish, and soon after the boy left home. He squandered his riches on wine and women and temporary pleasures, until one day he found himself poverty-stricken, hungry, and barely able to earn a living as a pig feeder.

Finally coming to his senses, the boy returned home in sorrow and disgrace, ready to beg his father to take him in again. And here comes the good part. The Bible says:

"So he got up and went to his father. But while he was still a long way off, his father saw him and was filled with compassion for him; he ran to his son, threw his arms around him and kissed him.

"The son said to him, 'Father, I have sinned against heaven and against you. I am no longer worthy to be called your son.'

"But the father said to his servants, 'Quick! Bring the best robe and put it on him. Put a ring on his finger and sandals on his feet. Bring the fattened calf and kill it. Let's have a feast and celebrate. For this son of mine was dead and is alive again; he was lost and is found.' So they began to celebrate" (Luke 15:20–24 NIV).

Two things strike me about this father: 1) He loved freely, and 2) he loved continually.

The son in this story certainly had been wrong—sinfully wrong—in his treatment of his dad. Yet the father never required a repayment for the wrongs, never demanded the boy work to pay back all the money he'd squandered. This father's love was free—no strings attached. The father loved unconditionally, with no thought of personal gain in return. He loved freely!

He also loved continually. Notice that the whole time the son was out wasting the dad's money, the father never stopped loving the son. In fact, when the child finally came home, who was the first to meet him at the door and welcome him with an embrace? The father. Years and distance couldn't weaken the father's determination to love his son. His love was never ending.

Now, imagine if you and I loved like that. If you and I let God's Holy Spirit enable us to love others a bit more freely and continually each day of our lives. If that free, persevering love characterized our every thought and deed, our every attitude and action.

Truth is, if we could learn to love like that, then Jesus' prayer, "Hallowed be Your name," would become more than words to be repeated. It would be a fact that happens day in and day out in your life and mine.

FOR FURTHER REFLECTION. . .

Blessed be the name of the LORD from this time forth and forevermore! From the rising of the sun to its going down, the LORD's name is to be praised.   PSALM 113:2–3

"Praise be to the name of God for ever and ever; wisdom and power are his. He changes times and seasons; he sets up kings and deposes them. He gives wisdom to the wise and knowledge to the discerning. He reveals deep and hidden things; he knows what lies in darkness, and light dwells with him."   DANIEL 2:20–22 NIV

All the nations—and you made each one—will come and bow before you, Lord; they will praise your great and holy name. For you are great and perform great miracles. You alone are God. Teach me your ways, O LORD, that I may live according to your truth! Grant me purity of heart, that I may honor you. With all my heart I will praise you, O Lord my God. I will give glory to your name forever.

PSALM 86:9–12 NLT

4

YOUR
KINGDOM COME

We're nearing the halfway point to this little book, and I'm going to do something just a bit different from the rest of this book. You see, I've been rereading the next portion of the prayer of Jesus—three little words, really:

"Your kingdom come. . ."

I'm struck by this simple phrase and the implications of it for you and me. Scottish theologian, John E. McFadyen, sheds light on this portion of the prayer of Jesus, saying, "The kingdom of God [is] in its essence a moral and spiritual kingdom. . . . [This] prayer is essentially a petition for the triumph of the cause of God in the world—of truth, and goodness, and love."[1]

So when Jesus prayed these words, "Your kingdom come," several truths were in play. First, Christ Himself, while He walked the earth, was the physical embodiment of God's kingdom on earth. As *Nelson's New Christian Dictionary* explains it, "[The kingdom of God is] a messianic kingdom in which Christ is auto-basileia, the kingdom of God in person."[2] In that sense, Christ's prayer was answered even as He prayed it. God's kingdom *has* come—and its name is Jesus Christ.

Second, I'm intrigued by the fact that although God's kingdom has come (past tense), it also will come (future tense). That is, when Jesus returns for His second coming, the kingdom of God will literally come (again) to Earth. At that time, the book of Revelation instructs, God will take His kingdom beyond the spiritual realm and set it up physically in our midst.[3]

Now, to be honest, I could write for pages about either of the two truths I just mentioned. But I find myself irresistibly drawn to the third truth encapsulated in that phrase, "Your kingdom come. . ." That is this:

Christ embodies the kingdom of God—and likewise, the Spirit of Christ is embodied within the hearts of each of God's children.

Do you see what that means? In the spiritual sense, the kingdom of God is come (present tense). Christ in us makes it so. And, by God's transforming grace, His kingdom knows no borders. It comes and goes wherever we Christians come and go.

Yes, God's kingdom has come (Jesus' first coming); yes, God's kingdom will come (Jesus' return). But as stirring as both those events are, we must also remember that the kingdom of God also *is* coming, continually in the present tense, as the Holy Spirit empowers and accompanies us through each day of this life. That is exciting!

And here's where I find myself departing from the norm, because part of me wants to get on my soapbox and begin dissecting all the implications of these three truths about the kingdom of God. Yet the more I pray over this chapter, the more I feel the need to focus primarily on this last truth—that God's kingdom is coming in and through each of us. And I feel that perhaps this midpoint in the book is a good time for me to step down for a bit—for this one chapter—and let something else do the teaching.

Now, don't worry, I plan to get right back on my soapbox in chapter 5! But for this chapter, will you let me simply tell you a few stories? Will you join me in hearing about how God's kingdom is being spread through the fingertips of people? Perhaps through these stories we both can grow a little deeper in our understanding of Christ's powerful words of prayer, "Your kingdom come."

THE ANGEL OF ANTIETAM[4]

Sometimes the kingdom of God shows up in the most unlikely of places—in the midst of the carnage of war. But when it makes an appearance, its touch is life changing. Consider the example of the Angel of Antietam. . .

The bloody battle of Antietam continued to rage near the barnyard that September day in 1862. It had all started when one of Robert E. Lee's Confederate commanders wrapped Lee's written orders around three cigars and stuck them in his pocket. The cigars—and the plans—fell out of the commander's coat and were later discovered by Union soldiers, who promptly turned them over to the northern General George McClellan.

The streets of America are paved with hot asphalt. The streets of New Jerusalem are paved with transparent gold. Jesus Christ teaches us how to walk on both!

JESS MOODY

With Lee's notes at his side, McClellan sent his army against Lee's men at Antietam on September 17, 1862. It was a furious, desperate conflict, so much so that 24,000 Americans died in battle, and many sources reported that the air around the battlefield became hued with a faint shade of red.

Which brings us back to the barnyard. While

the struggle continued between Lee and Mc-Clellan, many wounded soldiers were dragged, carried, and left in the relative calm at a nearby farm. As they lay, groaning, dying, and spent outside the big barn, many prayed, begging God for some kind of relief.

Suddenly, a horse and buggy pulled up, and a strange man exited. Going carefully from soldier to soldier, the compassionate stranger gave water and food to the hungry and thirsty men lying wounded on the ground. He gave his name to no one, and when he was finished, rode away and was never seen again. To this day, no one has ever been able to determine who that man was, but his presence brought hope and a measure of comfort to many hurting people caught in the midst of war.

Some soldiers fought this battle for the North; others fought for the South. But this man, who came to be known as the "Angel of Antietam," fought for an unseen ruler and enlarged the boundary lines of a different kingdom entirely: the kingdom of God.

KINGDOM ON THE STREETS[5]

Ricky Byrdsong walked this route to work nearly every day. As vice president of community affairs for Aon Corporation, the former college basketball coach figured he had the best job in the world.

"They're actually *paying* me to go to schools, talk to kids about what's important in life, and run basketball camps for inner-city kids in the summer," he used to say with a smile.

So each workday, Coach Byrdsong would trot down Wacker Drive in downtown Chicago, heading to his office in the mammoth building where the Aon Corporation was headquartered. One windy Chicago morning, Coach Byrdsong spotted a man sitting on a sidewalk across the street from the company's headquarters. His name was James Saunders, and he had lost both his legs due to infection caused by a stab wound in his back. Now he spent most of his days sitting in a wheelchair on Wacker Drive, begging each passersby for money.

"Got a dollar or two, Mister?" Saunders called out to the coach.

"Sure." A committed Christian, Byrdsong responded as he thought Christ would, dropping a $5 bill into the hands of the man. Most people just hurried off after that, but something caused Ricky to hesitate. "Say," he said, "losing your legs must be tough. What happened?"

So began a new friendship between the big-time, corporate VP, and the disabled panhandler.

Over the next several weeks and months, Ricky Byrdsong and James Saunders paused to chat with each other just about every morning. And each day, Ricky Byrdsong brought a little respect and joy into James Saunders's life, simply by taking the time to be his friend. Coach Byrdsong discovered how Saunders had spent the last twenty-five years in and out of hospitals, holding temporary jobs and suffering through three failed marriages. Saunders discovered how, after posting an unwanted losing streak, Ricky had been summarily fired as head coach of basketball at Northwestern University.

Ricky was impressed with the other man's dogged persistence—rain or shine—to show up for "work" on that sidewalk across the street from Aon. When James finally asked if there might be a job for him at Byrdsong's company, the coach said, "Can't promise anything, James. But I'll see what I can do."

With Ricky Byrdsong's recommendation to give him a start, James Saunders became one of the most reliable mailroom workers at Aon Corporation. But, thanks to the touch of the former coach, he'd landed more than just a job. He'd been given a chance to live life with dignity again.

KINGDOM AT HOME[6]

Sometimes we forget that God's kingdom often begins within the doors of our own homes. In his excellent book, Daily Disciples, *David Wardell shared a story about how he learned that for himself. With his permission, I'll let him share that story with you now. . . .*

Ironically, one of my biggest opportunities for personal growth came as a result of *my encouraging others* to be involved in committed relationships.

I was just beginning to go out and speak (representing Promise Keepers) throughout the state of Colorado. As I put together speaking material, I read a book that included a long listing of different ways men could show love to their wives. I had written up a synopsis of that material and copied down a list of one hundred items. Then I decided, "What better way to find out if this is 'on target' than to bounce it off my wife?"

One Saturday I wasn't out speaking and was spending the day at home for a change, so I said, "Carolyn, I want to run something by you." I asked her to rate me on a scale of one to ten as I read from the list of one hundred ways to show love. I told her I wanted to know "How am I doing?" As I started down the list—I had given myself tens obviously—I was in for a rude awakening.

I didn't get past the first few questions. Already, she was ranking me at about a two or a three. I stared back at her in disbelief, but after twenty-nine years of marriage, I knew when she wasn't kidding—and this time she was dead serious. Sitting over breakfast that day, I can remember being totally stunned.

But I couldn't deny the scores my wife had given me. She had *the look* in her eyes, as the character Tim Taylor from *Home Improvement* would say. It's a look you would know if you've been married for a long time. The one where your spouse just cuts right through you.

I could see this wasn't fun and games. Did I struggle on through the full list?

Nope.

I got through three items.

For the next two and a half hours Carolyn laid into me and made me feel about an inch tall—like I'd never done anything right my whole married life. She just unloaded. Obviously, she was pretty frustrated with my behavior. I searched for something to say in response; the only thought that came to me was that I had better just keep my mouth shut and listen. I didn't try to defend myself. I just tried to take it in quietly. When she was finally finished, I felt as if I'd been punched. . .knocked to my knees.

And here I was the person who was fixing to go out and challenge others.

My resolution to change allowed God to do something significant in my life. I began to do laundry, fix meals, do dishes—in short, I began to do a much, much better job *serving* Carolyn. I made a commitment to live this way every day, doing practical things to demonstrate my love for her. As a result, not only did my relationship with Carolyn change, but I also grew closer to the Lord. (After all, when we allow selfishness to come between others and us, it also puts us at a distance from Christ.) Through it all, my committed Christian friends helped hold me accountable. They helped me walk the daily path of discipleship. Carolyn, naturally, was the one who helped me most.

She came to me about four weeks later and said, "David, you a becoming a man of integrity—you are becoming a promise keeper." My heart soared. I'd never heard that, not from my father or anyone else close to me. But here was my wife of twenty-nine years, after just four weeks of my changed behavior, honoring me for my commitment. Her appreciation continued to replenish and refire my desire to serve her as

Christ had called me.

This was a real turning point in our marriage. I had always felt we had a good marriage, but apparently, from her perspective, it had been a rotten marriage. After all, I never did anything. To this day, however, with thirty-plus years of marriage now behind us, I can look back and see the turnaround in our relationship.

If we really take the gospel and live it out in every aspect of life, we transform that culture!

CHUCK COLSON

My wife and I are many things to each other—but one of these, certainly, is that we are fellow disciples who are there for one another; we disciple each other. The passage John 10:10 says, "The thief comes only to steal and kill and destroy; I have come that they may have life, and have it to the full" (NIV). I feel that our marriage has gone from what was a mediocre marriage, at least in my wife's perception, to an abundant, full, and blessed one. My only wish is that I had done things differently from the very beginning instead of waiting until I'd been married for twenty-nine years. These days, one of my greatest joys is daily living a disciple's life alongside my bride.

GOD'S KINGDOM
IN AUSCHWITZ[7]

Thirteen-year-old Sigmund Gorson huddled against the cold and tried to still the freezing tremors of fear that rumbled within him. Caught up on the wrong side of Hitler's Nazi Germany, Sigmund's parents had been torn from the boy and murdered, while the new teenager was imprisoned in the infamous Auschwitz concentration camp.

Lost and alone in a hostile world, the young man endured an existence devoid of family and overwhelmed by warlike oppressors. Everywhere he went, Sigmund asked the same questions:

"Please, did you know my father? Did you know my mother? Is there anyone who was a friend of the Gorson family? A neighbor? Please. . ."

In Sigmund's mind, if he could find someone who had at least known his family before this hardship, then he wouldn't be so terribly, utterly alone.

One day he came across a man in the prison. Balding, thin, but round-faced, and with piercing eyes, the man stopped Sigmund.

"Please, did you know my father?" the boy began. The man shook his head sadly.

"No," he said. But instead of leaving, the

priest stayed. And listened. The man was named Maximilian Kolbe, and he was a priest. Sigmund Gorson poured his heart out to the priest, asking for more than just someone with knowledge of his family. "Where is God?" he sobbed to Father Kolbe. "Why did He let my parents get murdered? I've lost my faith, Father. I've lost my faith!"

Sometimes the priest would speak comfort to the boy, but most often he would reach out tenderly and wipe away the tears while weeping with Sigmund at the same time. Day after day, the priest and the boy determined to live—and to love in spite of the terror of their lives.

Sigmund Gorson survived Auschwitz. Maximilian Kolbe did not; he was murdered by starvation and lethal injection by his Nazi captors. Yet years later, Sigmund still thanked God for the man who brought the touch of Christ and His kingdom into the filthy, cruel world of Auschwitz.

"He was like an angel to me," Gorson remembered. "Like a mother hen, he took me in his arms. He used to wipe away my tears. I believe in God more since that time. Because of the death of my parents, I had been asking, Where is God? and had lost faith. Kolbe gave me that faith back."

AN INVITATION TO THE DEVIL[8]

"If you sing about Jesus tonight and preach the gospel, we're going to hurt you!"

The voice on the other end of the telephone practically hissed into Steve Camp's ear. A Christian music artist, Steve had come to Canada to spread the news of God's kingdom to people living there. Along the tour, he'd encountered a group of devil worshipers who called themselves Satan's Choice. This group had held meetings at a university near the St. Catherine area of Eastern Canada. When news got out that Steve Camp was going to hold a concert at the same university, Satan's Choice was furious.

While the crew was setting up the stage for the concert, several received threatening phone calls backstage from this group, saying, "If this Christian singer, Steve Camp, sings about Jesus tonight, we're going to kill him!" During prayer before the concert, someone approached Steve with the news that the head of the satanic coven was on the phone wondering if Steve would take the call.

The singer put the phone to his ear and was immediately greeted with a threat on his life. The man informed Steve that he had fifty members in his coven and that if Steve sang about Jesus, they were "going to hurt" him.

The musician wasn't about to be deterred, however. He'd come to this Canadian university to sing about Jesus and to spread God's kingdom; no mere satanic coven was going to stop him.

"Take your best shot," Steve countered. "And, hey, if you're not doing anything tonight besides plotting my death, I'd like to invite you all to be my guests at the concert this evening."

There was a momentary silence, and then the caller asked, "How will we get in?"

Steve promised to leave fifty complimentary tickets to the show at the back of the auditorium for all "the visiting Satanists in the community."

That night, forty-five members of Satan's Choice came to the concert. They spent most of the time trying to be disruptive, throwing garbage on the stage and cursing. Finally, Steve Camp spoke, "In the name of Jesus Christ, sit down." And they all sat down.

Steve then presented a clear message about the hope of the gospel, about how Jesus came to earth, died on a cross to pay for our sins, and then was raised to life again and now offers eternal life to any who will ask and believe Him.

I'll let Mr. Camp tell you the end (new beginning?) of his little kingdom excursion into Canada that night. He reports:

"At the end of the invitation that evening, and I say this only in praise of our Lord and as a spectator of God's grace, thirty out of those forty-five Satanists received Jesus Christ as their Lord and Savior!"

AN ANGEL'S DRESS[9]

As John Eades reminds us in this story, sometimes God's kingdom lives in a broken-down trailer, right next door. . . .

Fannie lived in a run-down trailer surrounded by a lot of broken things. The stove only had one eye that worked, but that was all she needed to heat a can of pork and beans for her lunch and supper meals. The front door wouldn't close tightly, and her air conditioner had died during the last August heat wave. It was now December so she didn't mind that much, either. The television was a night-light but nothing more, and the mattress had springs that sagged like Fannie did when she lay herself down at night.

Fannie had gotten used to being surrounded by broken things, but it was the broken things inside of her that bothered her the most. She had a broken hip that was slow to heal and arthritic fingers that had forgotten how to work together; but, above all, it was her broken heart that hurt her the most. Her husband of forty-seven years had left her five years ago for a younger woman who had dollar signs—not love—in her eyes. He had made a fool of Fannie, and she had paid the price. Yet, it turned out he had made an even bigger fool of himself because his new wife ran around on him more times than a racing car does the track at the Indianapolis 500. It turned out that he had made a major mistake and that he would be paying forever the ultimate price, which was the loss of his childhood sweetheart, Fannie.

Fannie Albritton wasn't a complainer. She kept her feelings to herself and always had a ready smile for the children who lived in the trailer park where she did. It was a rural trailer park, and many of the children came from poor families. Perhaps, in a way, it was a city unto itself, where broken things and broken people had been drawn together by fate and circumstances. The middle of December had come and so did Diane Barnes, a nine-year-old neighbor of Fannie's, rattling the loose trailer door as she knocked.

The men who give themselves away—these are the freemen of the kingdom; these are the citizens of the new Jerusalem.

GEORGE MacDONALD

"Come in," yelled Fannie, "it's always open." She laughed at the truth of her words.

"Hello, Miss Fannie," Diane timidly said, opening the creaky door and entering.

"Well, what do I owe this pleasure to?" Fannie asked, as Diane stood there without moving, looking pretty much like a store doll in ragged clothes.

"Uh, I, er, uh, I was just wondering something, Miss Fannie," Diane stuttered.

"Well, Child, get it out before it chokes you," Fannie said.

"Yes, Ma'am, Miss Fannie," she replied, then started again. "Miss Fannie, I got selected to be one of the angels in the school play!" The words flew from her mouth.

"My goodness, my precious child, ain't that an honor," Fannie replied, motioning for Diane to come close to her chair. "I sure am proud of you. I suppose they decided to pick real angels this year," Fannie spoke as she smiled. Diane giggled and then became very quiet with her head facing the floor.

"You don't seem so happy, Child. What's the matter?" Fannie inquired as she adjusted her glasses and looked intently at Diane.

"Oh, Miss Fannie, I told a lie to my teacher, and now I don't know what to do," Diane hesitantly said with a concerned look upon her face.

"What kind of lie?" Fannie questioned.

"A big one," Diane answered in earnest. "The

teacher said we had to have silk and lace angel costumes with wings and everything, and I told her my momma could make mine, and it'd be no problem. You can't be in the play unless you have an angel outfit." Diane spoke and then fell silent. For a moment it seemed the whole world had stopped moving.

"What did your momma say?" Fannie asked, breaking the silence.

"She said we didn't have money to be throwing away on such foolishness, and I should just tell the teacher I didn't want to be an angel in the play. But, Miss Fannie, I do want to be an angel in the play. I want to more than anything in this whole world." Diane began to cry, and Fannie placed her hand on her shoulder and soothed her quiet. Then Miss Fannie rose from her chair and went into her bedroom and returned with a tape measure.

"Come here, precious child, and stand straight for me," Miss Fannie instructed, as she began to take measurements using a stubby pencil to jot them down on the inside cover of an old book lying next to her Chair. "You're going to be in that play, Child. I've been sewing my whole life."

Diane stood as still as a wooden soldier as Fannie completed her measuring. "Oh, thank you, Miss Fannie," she squealed as Fannie finished, "thank you so very much. I've got two weeks until the play. Can you really finish it by then?"

"Of course, Child. Now run on home. I've got work to do." Fannie shooed her away with her hands.

Diane's smile spread across the whole world as she jumped all the way home. Meanwhile, Fannie alternated between rubbing her arthritic fingers and her head as she pondered how she would ever get the cloth, much less get her hands to hold and push a needle.

Mr. Albritton had left behind a bunch of bad memories and a good tool set. Miss Fannie kept the pliers and sold the rest, using the money for lace and silk. Pointed scissors and pained hands cut the fabric from memory, not using a pattern. Miss Fannie stayed up late into the night, night after night, pushing and pulling the needle, using the pliers to grip it. Miss Fannie also used the pliers to shape the coat hangers into angel wings. Only a person with crippling arthritis could understand the pain Miss Fannie had to endure to complete Diane's angel outfit. All the stitches were tight, and the lace sleeves were the proper finishing touches. It was the most beautiful dress Miss Fannie's frail eyes had ever beheld.

Diane Barnes came by on Friday evening. The costume fit perfectly. "You look like a real angel," Miss Fannie exclaimed, and Diane beamed like the morning sun. "You'll be the hit of the play come Saturday night," Miss Fannie sincerely said. "Who knows, maybe I'll come, if I can get a ride to the school. Now run on home, little angel."

Sometimes going home isn't as good as it sounds. That night a human tornado came into the Barneses' trailer. Its name was "Red" Barnes, and he was drunk and destructive and, seeing the angel costume carefully laid out on the bed, he went berserk, thinking his wife had bought it. His mechanic's hands tore it into greasy pieces as he caused a terror that stopped even Diane's tears from flowing.

Miss Fannie got the word early Saturday morning, and holding a crying Diane, she told her to go on to the school that night with her momma, and she'd come later to be with her to watch the play. The Christmas pageant was to begin at seven o'clock that night in the school auditorium, and Diane sat in the audience nervously watching the front doors. She was afraid Miss Fannie wouldn't come and that her father would.

At 6:45, an old woman named Fannie Albritton came down the aisle of that country school auditorium with a large box balanced across the top of her walker. She would have been there sooner but couldn't get a ride, so she had walked over two miles before a kindhearted man heading to the play had stopped to give her a lift. Miss Fannie had spent all day cutting and sewing her old cherished wedding dress. She had used her hands because the pliers were too slow. The pushing and pulling of the needle brought pain to Miss Fannie, but not as great as the pain she had seen in Diane's face earlier that morning.

Diane cried with joy when Miss Fannie opened the box. "Run on and get dressed, Child! I came to see the prettiest angel of them all," Miss Fannie said. "I'll be right here watching you."

There isn't any doubt that God was watching that night, also. Surely He must have smiled, knowing that Miss Fannie Albritton would never need another angel outfit herself, seeing as how she already had one.

A KINGDOM STORY
OF YOUR OWN

Well, we could go on sharing stories like this for hours—and what a wonderful time that would be! But I think maybe it's time for you and me to turn our attention inward and ask another question:

If we are citizens of God's kingdom, how are

we spreading Christ to those in our world today?

Perhaps, like David Wardell, we should start in our own homes. Or like the Angel of Antietam we should seek out the hurting and offer comfort. Or like Maximilian Kolbe and Fannie Albritton, we should be drying the tears of heartbroken children. Or something altogether different. We're limited only by our willingness and God's grace to use us!

How about this? How about if we determine today—right now—to echo the prayer of Jesus, "Your kingdom come. . ."? And then let us determine, with help from Christ's Holy Spirit, to be agents of God who spread His kingdom with every fingerprint we leave behind.

May God make it so!

FOR FURTHER REFLECTION. . .

Again [Jesus] said, "What shall we say the kingdom of God is like, or what parable shall we use to describe it? It is like a mustard seed, which is the smallest seed you plant in the ground. Yet when planted, it grows and becomes the largest of all garden plants, with such big branches that the birds of the air can perch in its shade."

Mark 4:30–32 niv

"The Kingdom of Heaven is like a treasure that a man discovered hidden in a field. In his excitement, he hid it again and sold everything he owned to get enough money to buy the field— and to get the treasure, too!

"Again, the Kingdom of Heaven is like a pearl merchant on the lookout for choice pearls. When he discovered a pearl of great value, he sold everything he owned and bought it!"

Matthew 13:44–46 nlt

For the kingdom of God is not a matter of eating and drinking, but of righteousness, peace and joy in the Holy Spirit, because anyone who serves Christ in this way is pleasing to God and approved by men. Let us therefore make every effort to do what leads to peace and to mutual edification.

Romans 14:17–19 niv

5

YOUR WILL
BE DONE
ON EARTH AS
IT IS IN HEAVEN

The story is told of a man desperately seeking to know the will of God for his life. Hearing of a new method for discerning God's will, he decided to try the "Open Window" technique.

Diligently following the instructions he'd received, our hero carefully placed an open Bible by an unshuttered window, then stepped back to watch. In a moment, a stiff breeze blew through the screen, fluttering the pages of the Good Book. When the pages had settled again, our friend closed his eyes and plopped a finger down onto the text, confident that whatever verse his finger now touched would be one to reveal God's will for his life.

He peered expectantly at the Scriptures and found his finger on a verse that read, "Judas went and hanged himself."

A bit confused, the man decided he'd better

wait a moment longer; perhaps God wasn't finished turning the pages yet! Sure enough, no sooner had he set the Bible down again when another breeze sped by, leafing through even more pages.

Applying his prescribed finger once more, the man was a little dismayed to find this time the Scripture read, "Go and do likewise."

Unsatisfied (to say the least!), he opted to try this "Open Window" method one final time. The verse he landed on next? "Whatever you will do, do it quickly."

So the man shut the window![1]

We might chuckle at this little story, but it does help us to focus on the next request that Christ made in the prayer of Jesus:

"Your will be done on earth as it is in heaven."

Aah, God's will. That seemingly elusive, secret destiny God has planned for each of us. In the New Testament alone there are over two hundred references to God's will. As theologian Wayne Detzler explains, "Perhaps the most prominent reference [to God's will] is found in the Lord's Prayer. There Christ taught His disciples to pray for the fulfillment of the will of God on earth as it is in heaven, without any resistance (Matt. 6:10). The primary test of one's Christianity is a willingness to do God's will (7:21)."[2]

I think it's interesting that Christ included this phrase, "Your will be done. . ." in his model prayer for us. I mean, God's will would seem a given, right? After all, we are praying to God at the moment we speak those words. Yet, upon a closer look at my own prayers, I quickly realize the wisdom of Jesus' reminder for us to ask God to work His will in our lives. Too often my own prayers are filled with my will—not God's.

"Lord, please give me a new car."

"Jesus, please give me enough money to pay for my son's college education. (And if You'd throw in a few extra bucks for my retirement, that'd be great, too.)"

"Father, please help the Jacksonville Jaguars to win this game. If they lose, they might miss the playoffs!"

You get the idea. My sense of God's will in my prayers can often be woefully inept! Yet Christ brings that necessity to the fore, requesting, in essence, that our requests be ones that further God's will on earth.

I love the way British theologian Selwyn Hughes expounds on this concept. He says, "Prayer is cooperation with God. We must have done with the idea that prayer is bending God's will to our will; it is a bringing of our will into conformity with His will so that His will may work in and through us. When you are in a small boat and you throw out a boat hook to catch hold of the shore, do you pull the shore to yourself or do you pull yourself to the shore? . . . When we cooperate with God in His plans—and we are more likely to do that following prayer—then He cooperates with us in His power."[3]

I hear you thinking at me now. "That's all well and good, Mike," you're saying. "I agree whole-heartedly. I would happily follow God's will, both in prayer and in life. *But I don't know what God's will is for me!*"

Okay, okay, no need to shout. Keep reading, and I will tell you a secret about God's will you may never have heard yet!

GOD'S WILL IS NOT A SECRET (BUT IT MAY BE A MYSTERY)

Here's the secret (are you ready?):

God's will is not a secret.

Oh, sure, sometimes there may be a mystery as to how His will plays out in our lives (more about that later). But more often than not, it isn't God who obscures His will for us; it's we who do that. In fact, God has been remarkably clear on the matter. Listen to what Jesus says about His will for our lives:

" 'Love the Lord your God with all your heart and with all your soul and with all your mind.' This is the first and greatest commandment. And the second is like it: 'Love your neighbor as yourself' " (Matthew 22:37–39 NIV).

If you and I are missing God's will for our lives, it's not because He has withheld it from us. His desire for us is twofold: 1) that we love Him completely, and 2) that we love His children selflessly. Any and all decisions we must make in this life can be filtered through those two commands.

Let me explain it another way. Let's suppose that you and I are standing on a long, winding pathway. From where we stand, the path branches off in several directions. We can see partway down some of the paths—a marriage partner here, a job opportunity there, a home location a little farther down, and so on.

So how can we know which path God intends for us to take? Is it the career hiding down path number one?

> *"Faithful Christians pray, 'Thy will be done, on earth as it is in heaven,' and then proceed to enact God's will— love, justice, peace, mercy, forgiveness— in the present, on earth."*
>
> PHILIP YANCEY IN
> *Reaching for the Invisible God*

Or the potential spouse inviting us down path number two? The missionary journey down path number three? The college degree down path number four? Or any of the other dozens of possibilities in our lives?

The question to ask ourselves at this point is not, "Which of these directions should I take to be in God's will?" Instead, we need to prayerfully ask, "Which of these paths provides the greatest opportunity for me to increase in my love for God and my love for others?"

That's it. Sounds simple, doesn't it? That's because it is! We've spent too many years convoluting God's will into a "should I or shouldn't I?" kind of shell game that often leaves us conflicted with doubts and distracted and disabled from serving the will of God in our lives.

Listen to what Pastor Ray Pritchard has to say on the subject:

> *Certainty in decision making is hard to come by in a fallen world. It helps to remember that even if we are confused, God is not. Confusion is not a sin, especially if it causes you to trust in the Lord with all your heart. . . . Since God wants you to know His will more than you want to know it, He takes personal responsibility to see that you discover it.*

Knowing God's will is ultimately God's responsibility, not yours. . . . *Let me suggest what this really means:*

- *He can put you exactly where He wants you to be.*
- *He can arrange all the details years in advance.*
- *He can open doors that seem shut tight.*
- *He can remove any obstacle that stands in your way.*
- *He can take your choices and fit them into His plan so that you end up in the right place at just the right time.*
- *He can even take your mistakes and bring good out of them.*
- *He can take tragedy and use it for your good and His glory.*

All He needs—in fact the only thing He requires—is a willing heart. He just needs you to cooperate with Him.[4]

Some of you are a bit annoyed with me (and with Ray Pritchard) right now, I can tell. *That's just too simplistic a way to view this complex life of mine,* you're thinking. *It can't be that easy.*

If that's what you're thinking right now, I won't argue with you about it. You go ahead and agonize over whatever you want to agonize over. Meanwhile, the rest of us will get busy living out God's will for our lives by finding those paths that facilitate best our love for Christ and for others! I'm confident that when you finally arrive at what you believe to be God's will for you, you'll be able to evaluate it then and realize that you've chosen the same things we have—you just took a little longer to get there!

What is God's will for you then? To love the Lord with all your heart, soul, and mind, and to love your neighbor as yourself. If your every action, your every thought and word, is filtered through this express will of God, then you won't need to desperately seek out His desires for your life; you'll have already found them.

GOD'S GREATEST DESIRE IS NOT TO MAKE YOU COMFORTABLE

Now, at this point I would be less than honest if I avoided a discussion of another aspect of God's will for our lives—that of pain. This is a lesson I've learned the hard way, and it's one I hope you won't have to learn with difficulty like I did.

When we pray Christ's words, "Your will be

done on earth as it is in heaven," we must also be willing to acknowledge a hard truth about God and His will.

God's greatest desire is not to make us comfortable in this life; it's to change us into the image of His loving Son, Jesus Christ.[5]

That means Jesus is often willing to let us endure annoyances, hardship, and discomfort in order to bring about His greater purpose in our lives.

Children's pastor Larry Shallenberger had to wrestle with this truth in his own life recently when a group of arsonists set his church ablaze in the wee hours of the morning. As he and his fellow staffers struggled to rebuild and recover from this senseless act of hatred, they discovered that one of the arsonists was the teen child of a member of the church's staff.

> *I was in the central highlands in Vietnam when someone remarked about how the Christians suffer there. One Vietnamese Christian remarked, "Suffering is not the worst thing that can happen to us. Disobedience to God is the worst thing."*
>
> TOM WHITE

Months later, Shallenberger and his church were still reeling from the consequences of this attack—and Larry found himself asking hard questions about God's will in this regard. The result was an essay he titled, "The Holy Arsonist." He speaks so eloquently, I'll let Pastor Shallenberger finish the story himself for you now:

Winter has come, and our firestorm continues on. I haven't reached too many conclusions about what's going on at my church. Questions have replaced sentences in most of my prayers. I wonder "Do Satan and God ever brush hands as they both reach for the same tool?" *Both use fire for their purposes. Satan uses fiery times to disfigure, scar, and consume. God uses fire to purify, refine, and strengthen. But when you're in the middle of the fire, how do you know who lit the match?*

According to Reformed tradition, Satan is God's devil. I understand that. I know there's great value in knowing that God is sovereign and doesn't cause evil. This knowledge is valuable, but I think my greatest learning has come in understanding the nature of suffering. I used to view God's promises to use fire to transform us into Christ's image as a somehow automatic occurrence. If a Christian suffers, then inevitably Jesus' character will shine through that person when the flames subside.

My experience this year forced me to shed that myth. As the year dragged on, I noticed impatience and anger spilling into my relationship with my son Alex. Resentful thoughts toward my coworkers were all too common. Anxiety crowded out God's peace far too often. Change was occurring in me, but not anything I own as Christlike. I had to fight what was happening in me.

Fire is one of Satan's favorite tools because of its ensuing destruction. Yet fire is also one of God's favorite tools because fire accelerates spiritual change. In the physical realm, fire agitates molecules and speeds up chemical reactions. The same is true spiritually. The fire of suffering is a spiritual accelerant. Suffering speeds up the stuff of our character and makes us susceptible to change. We see the consequences of our spiritual decisions more immediately in a week of suffering than in a year of tranquility. Saints and sinners are forged in fire.

Whose fire is it then—God's or Satan's? The answer lies firmly in our response to suffering. God will keep his

promise to make me like Christ in this
time—when I choose to respond in a holy
fashion. The fire becomes God's when I am
humble and content with God's hand.

I have no answers for most of the
questions our church has now. There is
one answer I hope to be able to give,
though. When asked, "Who was behind
the arson at Grace Baptist?" I hope to be
able to answer, "It was God." [6]

How is God using Larry Shallenberger's experience to forge the image of Christ more deeply within him? I don't know that yet, and neither does Larry. But in the midst of this difficult time, Pastor Shallenberger is learning to trust God even while enduring the discomfort of His will. That's a lesson we'd do well to learn, also!

This whole experience reminds me of something that theologian A. W. Tozer once said about the mysterious aspect of God's will. He reminded us that so much of what God is doing in our lives happens without our knowledge, saying:

It is heartening to learn how many of
God's mighty deeds were done in secret,
away from the prying eyes of men or
angels. When God created the heavens and
the earth, darkness was on the face of the

deep. When the eternal Son became flesh, He was carried for a time in the darkness of the sweet virgin's womb. When He died for the life of the world, it was in the darkness, seen by no one at the last. When He arose from the dead, it was "very early in the morning." No one saw Him rise. It is as if God were saying, "What I am is all that need matter to you, for there lie your hope and your peace. I will do what I will do, and it will all come to light at last, but how I do it is My secret. Trust Me, and be not afraid."

With the goodness of God to desire our highest welfare, the wisdom of God to plan it, and the power of God to achieve it, what do we lack?[7]

These kinds of sentiments were not easy for Helen Roseveare to accept. A medical missionary from England, Helen was serving in the Congo when Mau Mau revolutionaries invaded. This woman, who wanted nothing more than to serve God and love others—and had committed her life to doing just that—was attacked by the invading soldiers. She was beaten, raped, and humiliated at the hands of her attackers. Yet she survived.

During her recovery from this traumatic

event, Helen struggled with God and how He might let something like that happen to her, His very own servant and child. Finally, after many tears and prayers, she wrote herself a note, a letter to herself from God.

"Can you thank Me for trusting you with this experience," she wrote, "even if I never tell you why?"[8]

We must learn to trust God, no matter what blessings and curses He wills into our lives. Like Helen Roseveare and Larry Shallenberger, we need to learn to daily sacrifice our desire to be "comfortable" in return for God's desire to mold us into His loving image. When we do that, we can pray in truth the words of Jesus and say to God, "Your will be done."

NO ONE IS EXEMPT FROM DOING GOD'S WILL

Before we finish this chapter, we need to recognize one last truth about God's sovereign will: No one is exempt from His plans and purposes, most especially those of us who call Him Father.

Think about it. Jesus Christ, when He walked the earth, was God incarnate; the one and only Son of God. Yet even He submitted Himself wholly to the will of the Father! Remember His trial in the Garden of Gethsemane? The Bible describes it this way:

> *Then Jesus went with his disciples to a place called Gethsemane, and he said to them, "Sit here while I go over there and pray." He took Peter and the two sons of Zebedee along with him, and he began to be sorrowful and troubled. Then he said to them, "My soul is overwhelmed with sorrow to the point of death. Stay here and keep watch with me."*
>
> *Going a little farther, he fell with his face to the ground and prayed, "My Father, if it is possible, may this cup be taken from me.* Yet not as I will, but as you will."

MATTHEW 26:36–39 NIV
EMPHASIS ADDED

Not even His deity exempted Christ from fulfilling the will of the Father for His earthly life—even though it meant a brutal, torturous death for His Son. The result? Eternal life, love, and forgiveness for all who will believe in the Son. I don't even like to imagine where my life would be if Christ had "opted out" of fulfilling that will of God!

Often, though, well-meaning folk around

us will try their hardest to disqualify us from God's plans for our lives. They think we're not ready, not talented enough, not "godly" enough. It reminds me of baseball legend, Yogi Berra.[9]

When Berra was in his early years of playing catcher for the New York Yankees, fans, writers, and even his own teammates made fun of Yogi. "Blessed" with what he calls a "stumpy" build, awkward looks, and a face that earned him the nickname, "the Ape," he took heat from all quarters! His own team manager, Larry McPhail, even reacted with disgust at Berra's looks, saying he resembled the "bottom man of an unemployed acrobatic team."

"I didn't look like a major league ballplayer," says Berra, "especially a New York Yankee, so I guess I was an easy target."

Yogi Berra could have quit then, figuring he'd gotten mixed up in the wrong racket. But he didn't. When fans, friends, and enemies belittled his appearance, he just shrugged and said, "So I'm ugly. So what? I don't hit with my face."

Several world championships—and legendary status—later, Yogi Berra is a household name for being a world-class baseball player and manager. I wonder what would have happened—what the sport of baseball would've lost—if he'd let all those other people convince him that he wasn't qualified to play ball for the Yankees?

And I wonder what we Christians are missing out on because so much of our society—including our well-meaning brothers and sisters in Christ—so often tell us we're not qualified to let God's will for our lives reign over each moment, each hour, each day of our lives. I think sometimes we'd disqualify even Jesus Himself if we had the chance!

I read a letter once that I think encapsulates beautifully our tendency to do just that kind of thing, and I want share it with you as we close out this chapter. It was written as a satirical response to Jesus' charge in Matthew 28:18–20 (NLT). In that passage He says, "I have been given complete authority in heaven and on earth. Therefore, go and make disciples of all the nations, baptizing them in the name of the Father and the Son and the Holy Spirit. Teach these new disciples to obey all the commands I have given you. And be sure of this: I am with you always, even to the end of the age."

To walk out of His will is to walk into nowhere.

C. S. LEWIS

Some enterprising soul composed this letter, highlighting how we (in our arrogant ignorance!) would probably respond to Christ today:

Dear Jesus Christ:

We acknowledge the receipt of Your recent communication.

Your proposal is both interesting and challenging; however, due to a shortage of personnel, as well as several other financial and personal considerations, we do not feel that we can give proper emphasis to Your challenge at this time.

A committee has been appointed to study the feasibility of the plan. We should have a report to bring to our congregation sometime in the future. You may rest assured that we will give this our careful consideration, and our board will be praying for You and Your efforts to find additional disciples.

We do appreciate Your offer to serve as a resource person, and should we decide to undertake this project at some point in the future, we'll get back to You.

Cordially,
The Christians[10]

Nothing—nothing! nothing! nothing!— should keep you from pursuing the will of God in your life. No committee, no "personnel shortage," no opinions of friends and family, no book (not even a book on the prayer of Jesus) should be allowed to interfere with your living out the words of Christ's prayer, "Your will be done on earth as it is in heaven!"

When you feel outclassed and unable to accomplish God's will in the way you love, the way you face trials, the way you participate in life's activities, remember, that's okay—but it doesn't have to keep you "out of the game." With Jesus by your side, no calling of God is too daunting, no failure is too great, no reason is reason enough for you to disqualify yourself from doing God's will.

So what are you waiting for? Let today be the day you finally pray the words, "Your will be done"—and then go out and live it as well!

FOR FURTHER REFLECTION. . .

While He was still talking to the multitudes, behold, His mother and brothers stood outside, seeking to speak with Him. Then one said to Him, "Look, Your mother and Your brothers are standing outside, seeking to speak with You."

But He answered and said to the one who told Him, "Who is My mother and who are My brothers?" And He stretched out His hand toward His disciples and said, "Here are My mother and My brothers! For whoever does the will of My Father in heaven is My brother and sister and mother."   MATTHEW 12:46–50

Do not conform any longer to the pattern of this world, but be transformed by the renewing of your mind. Then you will be able to test and approve what God's will is—his good, pleasing and perfect will.   ROMANS 12:2 NIV

"For I [Jesus] have come down from heaven, not to do My own will, but the will of Him who sent Me. This is the will of Him who sent Me, that of all that He has given Me I lose nothing, but raise it up on the last day. For this is the will of My Father, that everyone who beholds the Son and believes in Him will have eternal life, and I Myself will raise him up on the last day."   JOHN 6:38–40 NASB

6

GIVE US THIS DAY OUR DAILY BREAD

Hunger burned inside Bruce Olsen. It was the kind of hunger that felt like someone had taken a blowtorch to his insides, leaving his stomach worse than empty; it felt ravaged, angry, and achingly unfilled.

The young missionary took stock of his situation again. A month prior, he had made first contact with a tribe of South American Indians called the Motilones. That was when they'd shot him, sending an arrow piercing through his thigh. From there he'd been cruelly marched back to the Motilone camp where he was held prisoner while the Indians waited to see if he would recover from his wound.

When it became evident to Bruce that his leg wasn't healing, he escaped from the camp and began a long, limping trek back toward civilization. Unsure of his bearing, Olsen could only follow along a riverbank, hoping and praying it would lead him to people who could help.

Day one came and went, and Bruce was still

alone. Day two of walking produced only more of the same. His prayers for God's provision—of food, of medical help, of anything—seemed to reach no further than his barren existence. By day three, the young man was feeling weak, faint from hunger and exhaustion. Day four provided no relief, either, and Bruce began to feel delirious with hunger. I'll let him describe day five:

> *On the afternoon of the fifth day I wearily dropped into a seat between two huge boulders. . . . I looked at my fingernails, blue from the cold water; at my hands and fingers, pale white. My whole body groaned with pain; my stomach ached with hunger. I started to shake, and couldn't stop. I stared at the water, my gaze out of focus. . . . Could I go on any farther? I didn't see how. I needed food, rest. Something on the surface of the water seemed to be waving up and down, bright yellow. I couldn't make my eyes focus on it. I thought I was delirious. I rubbed my eyes. The water came into focus. Bobbing along in the current was a stalk of bananas. I grabbed them as they floated by. I couldn't believe it. . .as I began to digest them I felt them giving me strength and new hope. . . .*

God had given me a table in the middle of the jungle, a table of ripe bananas.[1]

A stalk of bananas, appearing out of nowhere, floating down a river until they're within reach of a weakened, hungry man? Yet another—albeit, dramatic—example of God responding to the sentiment expressed in the next portion of the prayer of Jesus.

"Give us this day our daily bread" is what Christ taught His followers to pray. For Bruce Olsen that phrase could have easily been changed to "Give us this day our daily bananas!" but the meaning is the same. By praying these words for us, Jesus reminded that it is God, not ourselves, who ultimately provides our daily needs. It's the same lesson He taught the ancient Israelites during the time of Moses, providing manna in the wilderness while they made their way to the Promised Land.[2]

One interesting observation about this portion of the prayer of Jesus is that this phrase, "Give us this day our daily bread," is the sole overt reference to any material thing in the entire prayer. All the other requests here have to do with spiritual things. That it ranks high enough in Christ's priorities to even be included in this model prayer speaks volumes!

The scope of this request is important to understand as well. As John McFadyen explains, "We cannot be too grateful for this simple recognition on the part of our Lord of the material basis of human life. . . . The petition is at once modest and comprehensive; it is not a prayer for prosperity, far less for luxury, but simply for that which makes life possible, and even that simply for the day—not for that abundance which will deliver us from anxiety for the morrow. But, on the other hand, it is implicitly a prayer for *all* that is needed to make life possible."[3]

> *When the Lord's Prayer says "Give us this day our daily bread," it means "Give us the basic material things we need today."*
>
> J. STEPHEN LANG

Theologian Ralph Gower adds, "Bread was so basic a food [in ancient Israel] that it became synonymous with life itself."[4]

So what was Jesus asking when He prayed, "Give us this day our daily bread"? He was asking for God to continue to sustain life itself in the believer; for our loving Father to provide the physical needs of our existence for yet another day. Now, let's discover more about what that means for you and me.

GOD CARES ABOUT
THE MUNDANE THINGS OF LIFE

Do a little experiment for me. Take a moment and try to recall everything you ate for dinner last night. Done? Now try to remember everything you had for dinner two nights ago. A week ago.

How'd you do? If you're like me, you might have gotten half of the items from last night's meal, and then drawn nearly a blank on anything before that. Yet God not only knows what you eat, He orchestrates the events of your life (and those of many others), including something so mundane as providing dinner for you.

Why would He go to that much trouble on your behalf? Simply because our God cares about the practical things of your life. Don't believe it? Then check out this passage of Scripture from Paul's letter to the Philippians: "Don't worry about anything; instead, pray about everything. Tell God what you need, and thank him for all he has done" (Philippians 4:6 NLT).

Friend, what do you think the Scripture means when it says "pray about everything"? Do you think it means, "Pray about everything, except which school your child should go to? Oh, and God's not really interested in whether or not you find a parking place, and He doesn't care much if you get stuck waiting in a doctor's office today, either, or how your favorite sports team is faring. He's not interested in whether or not you have the right ingredients for that pie you want to bake tomorrow or even if you'll have enough energy to get up before the snooze alarm goes off, either. Really, God's only interested in the 'big' things—you know, cancer, jobs, politics, that kind of stuff. All the rest is just a waste of His time."

If that's been your attitude toward prayer, you've missed out on—and underestimated—much of God's love and care for us. Those mundane moments our lives are consumed with are not off-limits to God! In fact, as is true in any real-life relationship, it's the boring, everyday, practical moments of the day that build intimacy. Why would you opt to keep those times away from the presence of God?

Christ didn't teach us to pray, "Give us this day our daily bread, unless You're too busy for that. 'Cause, you know, we can take care of that on our own and free up more time for You to stop a global holocaust or something."

No, Jesus taught that we can turn to God with our most humble, nitty-gritty requests for life—even for something as basic and practical as the food we'll eat today.

Julian of Norwich once said, "Not only does

He care for great and noble things, but equally for little and small, lowly and simple things as well. This is His meaning: 'Everything will be all right.' We are to know that the least thing will not be forgotten."[5]

I love the way Brother Andrew (the famous missionary who has spent decades smuggling Bibles into otherwise "closed" countries) has lived out this truth. It's something he calls the "Game of the Royal Way," and he learned it as a student at World Evangelism Crusade School in Glasgow, Scotland.[6]

As part of his course work, Andrew and four of his classmates were sent out on a four-week missionary tour through Scotland. The catch? They were each given just a British one-pound note to start their journey—and that one pound had to be repaid in full at the end of the tour! Additionally, the students were instructed that during their travels, they were not allowed to take up a collection or mention their needs to anyone other than God.

What do you think Brother Andrew prayed about during those four weeks? Sure, he probably prayed for success in his evangelistic efforts. He probably prayed for God's Holy Spirit to empower his preaching and bless his efforts. But he also prayed for all the mundane things he needed to keep his life going—for food, for a place to sleep, for clothing, for paper on which to write letters, for toothpaste with which to clean his teeth, and probably for a bathroom or two along the way!

And God answered all those prayers, providing homes (complete with bathrooms) in which to sleep, cash to purchase food and supplies, meals in churches, and more. Once God even provided a cake—mailed days prior—that was exactly what the students needed to fulfill a promise to have tea with some young people to whom they were ministering.

When they got back from this little tour, not only did they have double the amount of money needed to repay the one-pound loans, the group had also learned firsthand the power of praying, "Give us this day our daily bread."

In fact, after this trip, Brother Andrew once found himself out of laundry soap, something that cost eightpence in British coinage. Finding only sixpence in his pockets, Brother Andrew prayed for God to provide, then went to the store to buy soap anyway. When he got there, he found a sign in the window: "Sale on Laundry Soap! Twopence Off!" God had provided the way for Andrew to buy even something as mundane as soap!

We would all do well to realize this "Game of the Royal Way" is in reality no game at all.

God, our provider, cares about the mundane things in our lives. That's why we can pray with confidence Christ's words, "Give us this day our daily bread!"

GOD CAN BE TRUSTED WITH YOUR DAILY NEEDS

The question then, is not "Does God care about my daily needs?" It is, "Do I trust God to care for my daily needs?" That's where the rubber meets the road for most of us—even those known for having great faith.

I remember a story of famous missionary Gladys Aylward that illustrates what I mean.[7] This tireless worker lived and ministered in China in the early part of the twentieth century, creating a loving home for hundreds and hundreds of orphans.

At one point in her life, Japanese military forces invaded her home city of Yangcheng. With only one assistant and more than a hundred orphans in her care at the time, Aylward didn't know what to do. Finally, she and her assistant agreed they must take the children on a treacherous journey over the mountains to reach free China.

After they began the trek, Gladys felt the

impossibility of their situation settling in, and after a sleepless night in the mountains, she was ready to give up all hope of reaching their destination safely. That was when one of her orphans, a thirteen-year-old girl, came by her side and tried to encourage the missionary by reminding her of the Bible story about Moses and the Israelites crossing the Red Sea.

In despair, Aylward moaned to the girl, "But I am not Moses."

"Of course you aren't," the girl replied, "but Jehovah is still God!"

Gladys and all her charges made it safely over the mountains. Why? Because God is still God, and He can still be trusted—even when we don't feel like trusting Him to provide. That's so important it bears repeating:

God can be trusted with our daily needs!

Now, I can certainly tell you of many more wonderful stories about how God has provided for His children time and again—myself included. In fact, I even wrote an entire book on the subject once![8] But at this point I want to lead us to the exciting part of this equation. It's this:

Sometimes God entrusts us with the opportunity to be agents of His provision for others.

Or, to put it another way, often the way

God provides is by encouraging us to touch others whom He's put into our lives—family, friends, coworkers, church family, strangers, and more.

Novelist Terri Blackstock once told me a story of how she was on the unique receiving end of God's provision through the hands of another.[9] During 1998, she and her husband opted to sell their house and work toward down-scaling their financial obligations. The result was positive, but it also left Terry feeling a measure of uncertainty and anxiety each new day—something she admits she wasn't handling well.

Many seem to think I am very poor. . . . I would not, if I could, be otherwise than I am— entirely dependent myself upon the Lord, and used as a channel of help to others.

HUDSON TAYLOR

"One morning," she says, "I was confessing my anxiety to the Lord and asking Him to help me overcome it. And I said that it would be so wonderful if I could just see the Lord's instructions to me in writing! I said it facetiously, because God doesn't work that way. Usually."

Later that same day, Terri received a letter from one of her fans. This reader had written to Terri a year prior to say she enjoyed one of the prolific author's many books, and Terri had sent a thank-you card in return. Now, out of the blue, the fan had sent another letter to her favorite author, a letter that, by God's timing, arrived on the same day that Terri had prayed for help to deal with her anxiety.

"She wrote to say that God had laid me on her heart," Blackstock reports, "and that she had been praying earnestly for me. She felt led to write and share her favorite verse with me—Isaiah 40:31: 'But they that wait upon the LORD shall renew their strength; they shall mount up with wings as eagles; they shall run, and not be weary; and they shall walk, and not faint' (KJV).

"I cried and laughed at the same time. I had asked for written instructions, and they had come in the mail that day! This lady knew nothing of my waiting. But God did. What love, that He would help me with my peace of mind by giving words to a woman who doesn't even know me, halfway across the country. What love, that He would anticipate my prayer before I prayed it and have her write it and put it in the mail in time to get there exactly on the day I needed it."

This aspect of God's provision is something we all need to learn. You see, when we pray Jesus' words, "Give us this day our daily bread," there's an important word we often overlook: *Us*. Christ never intended for His followers to go through this life alone; His presence is partly manifested on earth through communities of faithful people who join together to help each other make it through the vagaries of daily living.

Not long ago, I read about a tornado that hit my old hometown, a suburb of Oklahoma City, devastating anything in its path.[10] One of the overlooked aspects from the aftermath of this tragedy was the high school prom. Dozens of young girls who had previously been planning and shopping with delight for this special night, now found themselves digging out any belongings they could find from under the rubble of their former homes.

Students at crosstown rival Edmond North High School heard about these girls' situation and decided to respond to tragedy with extravagance. The student council jumped into action, making calls and requesting help for their sister schoolgirls. People all over joined in to help out.

Dorothy Kelly, owner of a formal wear shop in Oklahoma City, donated 125 prom dresses. A local tuxedo shop promised free tux rentals to guys who'd been affected by the tornado. Others donated more gowns; people brought in dozens of dress shoes, purses, costume jewelry, and even makeup.

In the end, more than six hundred prom outfits in all sizes—with accessories—had been collected. Seamstresses also donated their time to make needed, on-the-spot alterations to gowns for any girls who needed them. After volunteers set up the donations into a makeshift boutique at Edmond North High, the school sent a bus across town and picked up girls from the tornado-struck area, bringing them back to pick out their outfits for the junior-senior prom.

"A lot of people might say there's other important things to worry about," said Edmond North's student council president, Marilyn Klopp. "But for us, the prom is so important."

Through the hands of Marilyn and others like her, the junior-senior prom became a fresh reality for dozens of teenage girls who, like Cinderella, needed a dress to go to the ball.

Something similar often happens to those of us who call on God, our Father, to meet our daily needs. We present our worries to Him each day, and He in turn marshals the forces of His family—you and me—bringing His resources and us together to provide for each other under His loving direction. What a privilege it is for us to be part of His divine touch on humanity in these tangible, person-to-person ways!

Still, we must remember that there are more needs in this life than those we can see and feel. And that leads me to one last truth in which we can take comfort:

IN CHRIST, WE HAVE
PROMISE OF OUR DAILY
SPIRITUAL NECESSITIES, TOO!

In John 6:35 (NCV), Jesus said, "I am the bread that gives life. Whoever comes to me will never be hungry, and whoever believes in me will never be thirsty."

There is so much more to this prayer for daily bread than, well, daily bread! Yes, we need food and shelter and clothing and such to survive the physical demands of this life, but our greater need is for nourishment of the spirit; for health and sustenance to the core of our very being. Who can provide for that part of us? Only One: Jesus Christ.

And so we must realize that when we pray, "Give us this day our daily bread," we are praying for more than just physical necessities. If we are wise, we will also recognize that we can use that sentiment to ask for true, everlasting food for the soul; to ask for more of Jesus Himself to fill up our daily existence. After all, He alone is the bread of life!

In Christ we have all the "food" that our spirits need. In Him we have the means to satisfy the cravings of the inner person—cravings for love and peace and hope and the very presence of God.

> *You can make*
> *physical bread from*
> *wheat, rye, rice, barley,*
> *corn, even potatoes.*
> *Bread for the soul*
> *can come from*
> *only one source. Jesus.*
>
> ROBERT C. SHANNON

As we near the end of this chapter, let me tell you one last story to bring home this point. It is about a man who endured the loss of his wife as the result of a swift and tragic illness. After the funeral, he sat in a chair in his living room and refused to move from that spot.

"He needs someone to clean his house," said a well-meaning friend. "To help him sort through his wife's belongings." So several came over and handled that chore for him. Still, he sat, unwilling to venture beyond that chair.

"He needs food," said another. "You know how his wife used to cook for him." So the next day, friends brought over pots filled with stews and pans of turkey and casseroles. But all the food went uneaten, and the man sat unmoved.

"He needs money," said a third friend. "Imagine how those funeral expenses have strained his budget!" So they took up a collection and presented the man with a large check to cover his bills. And yet he still sat mired in his thoughts.

Finally, a fourth friend walked empty-handed

into the room. He said not a word but took a seat next to the widowed husband. The others watched through the window as the two sat, side by side, saying nothing. After a time, they noticed tears beginning to fall down the husband's cheeks, and those tears were mirrored on the face of the friend. In a moment, the husband buried his face on the shoulder of his friend and let the sorrow flow out of his entire body.

The friend still said nothing but held the husband tightly while he cried.

Before long, the crying was done. The widower sighed, dried his eyes, and stood.

"Thank you," he said quietly. "I needed that." And so he began to live again after the death of his wife.

Like this saddened husband, many times the physical resources of the world are simply inadequate. We have no need of more casseroles or fat wads of cash. We need the intangible: healing and nourishment for our souls; bandages for broken spirits. In those times, it's comforting to know we can ask God for our daily bread, and He will provide the bread of life to bring new health to our inner beings.

"Give us this day our daily bread," Jesus taught us to pray. Thanks be to God that He is also willing to answer that prayer with Himself.

FOR FURTHER REFLECTION. . .

Then Jesus said to his disciples: "Therefore I tell you, do not worry about your life, what you will eat; or about your body, what you will wear. Life is more than food, and the body more than clothes. Consider the ravens: They do not sow or reap, they have no storeroom or barn; yet God feeds them. And how much more valuable you are than birds! Who of you by worrying can add a single hour to his life? Since you cannot do this very little thing, why do you worry about the rest?

"Consider how the lilies grow. They do not labor or spin. Yet I tell you, not even Solomon in all his splendor was dressed like one of these. If that is how God clothes the grass of the field, which is here today, and tomorrow is thrown into the fire, how much more will he clothe you, O you of little faith! And do not set your heart on what you will eat or drink; do not worry about it. For the pagan world runs after all such things, and your Father knows that you need them. But seek his kingdom, and these things will be given to you as well.

"Do not be afraid, little flock, for your Father has been pleased to give you the kingdom."

LUKE 12:22–32 (NIV)

I have been young, and now am old; yet I have not seen the righteous forsaken, nor his descendants begging bread. PSALM 37:25

And my God will supply all your needs according to His riches in glory in Christ Jesus.
PHILIPPIANS 4:19 NASB

7

AND FORGIVE US OUR DEBTS, AS WE FORGIVE OUR DEBTORS

In her endearing book *Heavenly Mail,* my friend Philis Boultinghouse imagines what it might be like if we could actually mail a letter to God—and receive a note back from Him in response. With her permission, I'd like to start off this chapter with one of her "exchanges" with God:

Dearest Father,

I come before You with a growing problem. Every day, the weight of my burden gets bigger and bigger. It's getting to the point where I'm crippled by the guilt I feel over past wrongs. I've hurt so many people, I've lied, I've lived selfishly, and I've made sinful choices—lots of them. And now, Lord, it's all catching up with me.

I've come to know You and Your saving grace in the form of Your Son, Jesus, but for some reason, I have a hard time believing that His grace can really apply to me. I believe that Jesus is Your Son, I've confessed my sins (that took a really long time, and I know I missed many), I have truly repented from my heart, and I was baptized in the name of Your Son. But I still have a hard time accepting that my sins could be so utterly and completely forgiven. To think that my sins could be instantly forgiven because I place my faith and trust in Your Son—it all seems too good to be true.

I want to feel the peace of absolute forgiveness, but I don't know if I dare let down my guard and bask in Your forgiveness for fear that I've not done enough to deserve it.

Please show me the truth of this forgiveness. I long for the peace it could bring. I eagerly await Your reply.

Your Guilt-Ridden Child

Here is the response from heaven:

Dear Guilt-Ridden Child,
Don't worry that the process of your forgiveness was too simple. To the contrary,

it cost Me the one thing most precious to Me in all the universe—it cost the life of My only Son. From days of old, I have set My heart upon bringing about complete forgiveness to those who trust in Me.

What can you say in response to My great love for you? If I am for you, who can be against you? If I did not spare My own Son, but gave Him up for you, will I not also graciously give you all that you need? Who is there who can bring a charge against you, My chosen one? I am the one who justifies. Who can try to condemn you? Jesus is the one who was raised to life and now sits at My right hand interceding on your behalf.

Though you can never earn the forgiveness that I freely offer to you in My Son, I do ask that you live in humble acceptance of what I have given you and that you share this forgiveness with others. You must confess your sins, openly and honestly. You must never claim that you are without sin. You must understand and believe that forgiveness comes only through the shedding of My Son's blood. And you must have a continual attitude of forgiveness toward all others who sin against you.

> *The peace of forgiveness is already
> in your possession. Let it freely wash over
> your soul.*
>
> *Your God of Forgiveness* [1]

What a beautiful introduction to the next portion of the prayer of Jesus! In her imaginary letters, Philis has hit the core of what Jesus' words mean when He prayed, "and forgive us our debts, as we forgive our debtors," in His model prayer. Referring to sins that we ourselves commit as well as to those committed against us by others, this plea to God reminds us that forgiveness is a gift we both receive and give—and one that's lavished on us freely (but not cheaply!) by God.

According to theologian Wendell Johnston, two words are used in the original languages of the New Testament to indicate forgiveness.[2] One is *aphiēmi,* and it means, "to send away." The image here is that of Jesus Christ picking up the wrongs we've done and then *hurling* them into nonexistence. (Something the Old Testament refers to by saying God has sent our sins "as far as the east is from the west" [Psalm 103:12].)

The second word the New Testament uses for forgiveness is *charizomai.* According to Johnston, this expression means, "to show favor, to pardon." It's a judicial term that indicates one is guilty of a crime—yet allowed to go unpunished.

And that's what happens when we pray Christ's words "forgive us our debts." (Or, as the reader-friendly New Century Version of the Scripture translates it, "Forgive us for our sins, just as we have forgiven those who sinned against us" [Matthew 6:12]). With those simple words, we ask God to perform a miracle, flinging our sins like a cosmic baseball so far away they cease to exist, then absolving us of the required punishment for those sins.

How can He do this? Simple, because the man who first prayed these words is also the Son of God who sacrificed Himself (through His death on the cross) to pay the penalty for our sins.[3]

There is nothing you have done that cannot be forgiven. Isn't that astonishing? Grace for the vilest, grace for the weakest, grace for the least, the last, and the lost.

SELWYN HUGHES

So now we have access to this miracle of forgiveness. And what are the results? Nothing short of complete transformation!

FORGIVENESS TRANSFORMS THE FORGIVEN

If you'd met John Newton in 1747, chances are you would've hated him.[4]

A self-described "wretch," he was at that time captain of a slave ship, making his living through the suffering of others. As a slave trader, John was involved in the kidnapping of African men, women, and children. Once they were captured, John would pack these people like lumber into the cargo hold of his ship, chaining them to posts within the hold. There, they'd be forced to endure a tortuous journey for weeks across the sea. Many people died at John's hands; many others went insane while trapped inside the cargo hold.

Those who survived didn't receive John's mercy, only his contempt. Upon arrival back at his home in England, John brought out his captives and sold them into a lifetime of slavery without giving a second thought to the many lives he was destroying in the process. Once his cargo hold was empty, John would take his crew and repeat the story all over again.

Kidnapping. Torture. Murder. Forced slavery. John Newton was guilty of all these crimes. And what's worse, he didn't even care.

Then the unthinkable happened. During a violent storm at sea, John Newton came face-to-face with death—and met God in His power. But instead of feeling the sting of God's judgment, he encountered the healing salve of God's forgiveness. And John Newton was never the same again.

Kidnapper. Torturer. Murderer. Slaver.

God forgave John Newton of all these crimes—and for the sin of a hardened heart. As Newton reveled in this forgiveness, he also realized the truth of his sin and the horrible suffering he'd caused by his own hands; and that made him sick over how he'd wasted his life.

He gave up his career as a slave trader, and the power of forgiveness slowly transformed every aspect of his life. Once hateful and cruel, he became thoughtful and kind. Once knee-deep in the business of human suffering, he joined with men like William Wilberforce and worked tirelessly to make the slave trade illegal in Great Britain. Once opposed to anything Christian, he himself became a minister and even a Christian songwriter who penned the now-famous words, "Amazing grace, how sweet the sound, that saved a wretch like me."

If you'd met Zacchaeus a few thousand years ago, chances are you would've hated him, too.[5]

For starters, he was a thief and a traitor. In fact, he was head of a group of thieves and traitors. Although a Jew, he had turned against his home and joined the forces of the conquering Roman government—as a tax collector, no less!

In this role, Zacchaeus preyed upon his own countrymen, demanding payment of taxes for Rome, collecting more than was required, and pocketing more than his fair share of the money.

For this kind of treason and graft, he'd become a very rich—and hated—man.

Yet, there came a day when Jesus Christ Himself came to Zacchaeus's hometown. Curious, the traitor scrambled up a tree to see the passing Messiah and soon found himself staring into the eyes of God. In those eyes of Christ, Zacchaeus deserved to see anger and wrath.

What he found there was forgiveness, complete and absolute.

You know the rest of the story, don't you? Jesus came to Zacchaeus's house that day, and the traitorous thief was transformed by the power of Jesus' forgiveness. Before Christ left, the greedy, cheating little man had become an honest, generous one. Forgiveness had brought what nothing else could: a change from the inside out.

Now, I could go on and tell you more stories about the transforming power of forgiveness— there are millions of them! But I'm hoping you, too, have experienced that firsthand yourself. I know I have! Back on July 15, 1980, God took an arrogant, prideful, former petty-criminal, religious hypocrite, teenager and hurled his sins to a place beyond access or comprehension. And now, decades later, I still feel the power of His forgiveness in my life, moment by moment, hour by hour, day by day.

Yes, forgiveness transforms the forgiven. I

(and hopefully you) are living proof of that. But, by the grace of God, the power of forgiveness doesn't stop there. Curious to know why? Then read on, read on!

FORGIVENESS TRANSFORMS THE FORGIVER

One of the beautiful things about the transforming power of forgiveness is its ability to change everyone involved. When God washes His forgiveness over the life of a man or a woman, He not only answers the first part of this section in the prayer of Jesus ("forgive us our debts. . ."); He also empowers us to fulfill the second part of that phrase (". . .as we forgive our debtors"). When that happens, we are changed by the act of forgiving almost as much as we are by the act of being forgiven.

Let me tell you another story to explain what I mean. This one is about Louis XII, king of France.[6]

Before Louis became king, there was uncertainty as to whether or not he would even live long enough to be a king. That's because his cousin, Charles VIII, was king of France first, and he viewed Louis as nothing more than a threat to his own rule. So Charles falsely accused his cousin of crimes against the throne and then had him thrown into prison. There, Louis lived a meager existence, kept chained in his cell and in constant fear of death at the hands of his cousin.

When Charles VIII died, however, Louis was released and crowned Louis XII, king of France! The new king's friends and advisors immediately recommended that Louis seek revenge on the former king's allies who had supported Charles's shameful treatment of him.

And so the king of France took out a pen and made a list of the names of all the men who had conspired against him and sent him to prison. Next to each name, the king carefully lettered a red cross on the parchment. When Louis's enemies heard of that red cross, they panicked, certain it meant they'd been sentenced to death on the gallows. Many actually fled the country rather than face the new king's wrath.

Then King Louis XII called for a special session of his court. When everyone was gathered, he spoke these words, "Be content and do not fear. The cross which I drew by your names is not a sign of punishment but a pledge of forgiveness and a seal for the sake of the crucified Savior, who upon His cross forgave all His enemies."

In performing this act, King Louis XII not only solidified his kingdom, he allowed forgiveness to change him, from a man whose natural tendencies would be vengeance, into a man who chose to show love. The power of forgiving had changed him so much so that it made him a friend to his enemies—and thus made many of his enemies into his friends.

You see, forgiveness transforms the forgiver by erasing the need to harm, to carry hatred in the heart, to let bitterness envelop what would otherwise be a joyful life. Educator and writer Hannah More once explained it this way, "A Christian will find it cheaper to pardon than to resent. Forgiveness saves the expense of anger, the cost of hatred, the waste of spirits."[7]

Forgiveness also works to transform us into the image of the great forgiver—Christ Himself! As hymn writer Alice Cary pointed out, "Nothing in this lost world bears the impress of the Son of God so surely as forgiveness."[8] Or, to put it in the words of an anonymous poet:

We are most like beasts when we kill.
We are most like men when we judge.
We are most like God when we forgive.

A redeemed slave named Caesar experienced this transforming truth firsthand.[9] As a child in the 1800s, he was kidnapped from his home in Africa and forced into slavery, ultimately serving a master in the West Indies. While in backbreaking service to a plantation owner, Caesar met—and experienced the forgiveness of—Jesus Christ. Caesar continued to be a slave, but his heart had been set free.

After years of grueling service as a plantation worker, Caesar finally earned his freedom. Though a freeman, the former slave chose to continue to serve his master, now as a worker for hire.

One day the master took Caesar to the slave market with him to purchase more slaves to work on his plantation. The owner searched the lot, bought the slaves he wanted, and then prepared to leave. He was surprised to hear his assistant begging him to stop. Caesar had spotted a tired old man on the slave block and was now pleading with his former master to buy this old slave.

"Why, Caesar, should I buy him?" said the slave owner. "Of what use can he possibly be?"

But Caesar was undeterred. "Please, Sir," he insisted, "you must buy him for me."

So the master gave in and purchased the useless old slave, giving him to Caesar to do with as he willed. Soon after, the old slave fell ill, and everyone on the plantation could see Caesar devoting any spare time he had to making the old man comfortable. He waited on him hand and foot, spoke kindly to him, and even washed the old man because he was too sick to wash himself.

Caesar's old master was moved by the compassion with which his former slave treated the old man. Finally he asked, "What connection do you have with that old man? Is he perhaps your father?"

"No," Caesar answered. "He is not my father."

"Well, is he some old friend or relative?"

"No," replied Caesar. "He is no relative of mine."

"He must be your friend then."

"No, Master, he is not my friend."

"But who in the world is he?"

The former slave spoke calmly. "He is my enemy."

The old man was actually the same person who had kidnapped Caesar from his parents' home and sold him into slavery! Yet, empowered by Christ's forgiveness of his own sins, Caesar chose to forgive the slave trader—and found himself transformed with compassion for the old man as a result.

Have you experienced this kind of freedom,

the power that comes from forgiving another? It's not likely you've been enslaved, but perhaps like Caesar and King Louis XII, you've been imprisoned or cut off or hindered or harmed by the actions and attitudes of those around you. Perhaps you've been lied to, insulted, stolen from, cheated, physically hurt, verbally abused, or any of a million things that people do to bring pain to each other. Now, I'm not suggesting you should dive headlong back into a situation that can cause you harm or make you unnecessarily vulnerable to abuse. But I am saying that you don't need to add to the pain you've experienced by refusing to forgive. To do so simply tightens the chains of bitterness and grief around your soul.

The shackles of your hurtful experiences aren't ones you have to wear; they're merely the bonds of unforgiveness. Why not loose their hold on your life? Why not join God in casting those hurtful sins of others as far away from you as possible? Why not ask God to empower you to experience the transformation that comes from forgiving others who have harmed you?

And why not do it today?

FORGIVENESS TRANSFORMS
OUR WORLD

There's one last truth in which we can rejoice
regarding this topic. You see, when we allow God
to empower us to forgive, we become more than
forgiver and forgiven ourselves; we become agents
of God's transforming power as it quietly invades
our world with compassion and kindness. We
become part of a revolution fueled by God's Holy
Spirit that literally changes our world, one person
at a time.

Prison Fellowship founder and former political power broker Chuck Colson tells a story
of how this revolutionary power of forgiveness
helped change an entire country. Listen as he
relates that story here:

*I was in Czechoslovakia a few years ago,
and I wanted to meet one man more
than any other. His name was Vaclav
Maly. He was the Catholic priest who in
1981 had been defrocked for preaching
the gospel and dispatched by the
Communists to clean the toilets in the
subway system of Prague. But on Christmas Eve, 1989, when the crowds began
to move out into the street, when it looked
like, finally, the Communist behemoth*

was to be overturned, the crowd started chanting, "Maly! Maly!" Up out of the subway came Vaclav Maly, the defrocked priest. He led them down to the main square of old Prague, and, as the New York Times wrote, eight hundred thousand people gathered around while Maly administered a service and offered forgiveness to all the Communists. All they had to do was come forward and repent. They did by the hundreds! The next morning, the tanks were gone. It was the velvet revolution; not a single drop of blood was shed. Maly was the hero of the velvet revolution.

Vaclav Havel, who became president of the country, called Maly in one day and said, "Father Maly, you can be anything you want in this government, from prime minister on down." Maly said, "Oh no! I just want to preach the gospel. I just want to tell people about Jesus." And so he went back to his church.

When I visited there in 1991, I wanted to meet him. I went to the Reform pastor who was my host and said, "Do you happen to know Vaclav Maly?"

He said, "Everybody in Czechoslovakia knows him, but I know him because we pray together every week for thirty minutes."

And so he took me to Maly's house. It was a little, gray, grubby building on the outskirts of Prague up on the side of a hill. There were five mailboxes and buttons, and one said, "V. Maly." Here he was, one of the most famous men in the world— "V. Maly." I pressed the button, and down to the front door came this man about forty years old. His face might have been chiseled out by Michelangelo, framed in beautiful, curly black hair, and with a wonderful, radiant smile. Within seconds we were embracing. Then I went up into his little apartment—a tiny little place shared with his father. On the table was mail from all over the world, and the telephone rang constantly. Nevertheless, we sat and had the most wonderful forty-five minutes of fellowship.

As I left, I turned and said, "I want you to know what a hero you are to many of us in the West."

His answer to me has changed my view of Christian service ever since. He said, "Oh no, Chuck! I am not a hero. A hero is someone who does something he doesn't have to do. I was simply doing my duty." [10]

For nearly a decade, Communist leaders made Vaclav Maly's life miserable. Yet this priest's unwavering dedication to do his "duty" to forgive his oppressors ushered in what Colson called a "velvet revolution"—a liberating war that was won without a single shot being fired.

Now, you and I may not find ourselves in a position like Father Maly, with eight hundred thousand people gathered around to witness our example of forgiveness. (Thank goodness!) But you and I can still be God's agents of forgiveness in our world—in the lives of those people within our sphere of influence.

What is forgiveness? It is the odor the flowers give off when they are trampled upon.

ANONYMOUS

In our families; in our workplaces; in our churches; in our communities; in our political organizations; in our clubs and athletic leagues; and in any other place where we come in contact with people, we can, like Vaclav Maly, be ministers of God's grace and forgiveness, and in so doing we can assist God as He transforms the hearts and lives of others.

That's what can happen when we join with Christ to pray His priorities, when we say from the heart, "And forgive us our debts, as we forgive our debtors."

FOR FURTHER REFLECTION. . .

Some people brought to Jesus a man who was paralyzed and lying on a mat. When Jesus saw the faith of these people, he said to the paralyzed man, "Be encouraged, young man. Your sins are forgiven."

Some of the teachers of the law said to themselves, "This man speaks as if he were God. That is blasphemy!"

Knowing their thoughts, Jesus said, "Why are you thinking evil thoughts? Which is easier: to say, 'Your sins are forgiven,' or to tell him, 'Stand up and walk'? But I will prove to you that the Son of Man has authority on earth to forgive sins." Then Jesus said to the paralyzed man, "Stand up, take your mat, and go home." And the man stood up and went home.   Matthew 9:2–7 NCV

Then Peter came to Jesus and asked, "Lord, how many times shall I forgive my brother when he sins against me? Up to seven times?"

Jesus answered, "I tell you, not seven times, but seventy-seven times."

Matthew 18:21–22 NIV

But if we confess our sins to him, he is faithful and just to forgive us and to cleanse us from every wrong. . . If you do sin, there is someone to plead for you before the Father. He is Jesus Christ, the one who pleases God completely. He is the sacrifice for our sins. He takes away not only our sins but the sins of all the world.

1 JOHN 1:9, 2:1–2 NLT

8

AND DO NOT LEAD US INTO TEMPTATION, BUT DELIVER US FROM THE EVIL ONE

"Everyone probably cringes when they think of one time or other during their lives when it would have been easy to have done the right thing and instead we do the wrong thing."

These words of a sixty-one-year-old man named Sergio ring especially true when you consider the source. After resisting a certain temptation for more than five decades, Sergio finally gave in. At the age of fifty-six, for the first time, he bought a sexually explicit video and brought it home.

Hey, he was a grown man, he reasoned. And he had needs just like everyone else. So why not indulge in this little indiscretion? After all, pornography is a multimillion-dollar business that "serves" millions of customers each day. If that many people do it, it couldn't be all *that* bad, could it?

So he gave in to temptation and bought the tape. A movie with little in the way of a story, but a lot in the way of sex and nudity. "That was the beginning," Sergio reports now. It was the start of a downward spiral into an obsession with sex that affected every area of his life.

Five years later, Sergio is a prisoner to his temptation. "I'm an older man, sixty-one," he says, "addicted to sex, online porn, and XXX videos—and my insatiable appetite doesn't show any signs of dwindling. I regret that I am unwilling, and therefore, unable to shake this as it consumes me. . . ."[1]

William McMullen faced a different kind of temptation—a temptation to tell a white lie. He needed a job (really, doesn't everyone?), and was eager to land one in a manufacturing plant. Added to this was the fact that people had told him he bore a remarkable resemblance to Notre Dame All-America halfback, Nick Eddy. So when asked his name during a job interview at the plant, McMullen gave in to temptation and passed himself off as Eddy. He got the job, but as McMullen says now, "I took a left turn when I should have taken a right turn."

You see, after building this work identity

as Eddy, it soon became his full-time identity. In fact, twenty years—several jobs, a wife and child—later he was still going by the name Nick Eddy. By this time, he'd used the Eddy name to secure a position as a high school football coach in Rochester, Massachusetts. McMullen had become so trapped in his new name and identity that he didn't even tell his wife and son about his name fakery!

Finally, in 1999, the real Nick Eddy discovered an imposter was using his name and put an end to it. But not before William McMullen's little temptation had turned into a lifetime of deception that brought pain and disgrace to himself, his wife and child, and dozens of others who had been wronged by the man's "white lie."[2]

These stories of Sergio and William McMullen bring us to the last portion of the prayer of Jesus—a phrase that both these men would have benefited from praying—and living:

"And do not lead us into temptation, but deliver us from the evil one."

Once again, Christ demonstrates a practicality in prayer that I find refreshing. We all face temptation—that is, we all deal with the "enticement to sin"[3]—each day of our lives. The certainty of temptation is as sure as the next breath you or I will take! And so Jesus finishes out this prayer with a practical plea for God to help us:

a) avoid temptation, and b) deliver us from Satan's tempting schemes.

Temptation is certainly nothing new—it's been around since the dawn of creation. The very first man and woman, Adam and Eve, became the first to succumb to temptation. Living in God's paradise, the Garden of Eden, they gave in to the tempter who, disguised as a serpent, convinced them to eat the forbidden fruit.[4]

On the surface, that temptation might seem a trivial one: Eat the fruit God has told you not to eat? What's the big deal about that? But, as theologian Henry Thiessen explains, that first temptation was not nearly that simple. Thiessen says, "Satan's temptation may be summed up as appealing to man in this way: It made him desire to have what God had forbidden, to know what God had not revealed, and to be what God had not intended him to be."[5] By going along with the temptation, Adam and Eve introduced sin into our world—and it's been with us ever since.

In exploring this further, Thiessen comments, "Sin is essentially selfishness. . .an exaggerated love of self, that puts self-interests ahead of God's interests."

So when we face a new temptation today, tomorrow, or ten years from now, we (like Adam and Eve) face a choice between God's interests and our own selfish impulses. Given

the track record of the human race, it's no wonder Jesus included the words, "And do not lead
us into temptation, but deliver us from the evil
one" at the end of His prayer!

By God's grace, we do not have to be constantly defeated by the power of the tempter.
We can daily experience God's answer to this
prayer in both big and little ways.

TEMPTATION IS NOT A SIN
(BUT IT'S ALWAYS A LIE)

The first thing we must understand about this
topic is this:

Being tempted is not a sin.

Listen to how Pastor Ray Pritchard explains
this truth:

> *Temptation is the common experience of
> all Christians. If you say, "I'll be glad
> when I'm not tempted," you're really say-
> ing, "I'll be glad when I'm dead" because
> you will be tempted as long as you are
> alive. Temptation changes shape across the
> years, but it never goes away completely. . . .*
>
> *Many Christians feel needless guilt
> because they have equated temptation
> with sin. Yet we know that our Lord was*

*tempted and was without sin (Heb.
4:15). Was the temptation real? The
answer must be yes. But if the sinless Son
of God could be tempted, then the temptation itself cannot be sinful.*[6]

Pastor Pritchard has hit the nail on the head
here. Why do we spend so much time agonizing
over the fact that we were tempted? It's wasted
time and energy. We're all tempted—even Christ
Himself was.[7] What matters is how we responded
to the temptation.

For instance, perhaps today you went to
church. While at church you saw a member of
the opposite sex all dressed up and looking fine
for the service. And the truth is, that person is
actually an attractive person. When you see that
person at church and acknowledge, even admire,
that person's beauty, is that sin? Of course not.
Beauty isn't a sin, and a refusal to acknowledge
beauty that God has created (such as in a Christian brother or sister) simply cheapens your life.

However, if after admiring that person's
beauty, you find
yourself falling into
a lustful fantasy star-
ring that person—
for instance, if that
dress looks so good on that woman that you start

*I can resist everything
except temptation.*

OSCAR WILDE

imagining her taking it off, or if that guy's muscled shirt makes you wish you could see what's underneath it—that's when the real temptation begins.

Your response at that point is what determines whether or not your admiration turns into sin. Do you deliberately direct your thoughts away from sexual fantasy? Good, you're resisting temptation. Or do you allow yourself to play out that sexual fantasy to its completion? In that case, you are allowing the tempter to lead you into sin.

That leads me to the second thing you need to know about temptation.

Being tempted isn't a sin, but temptation is always a lie.

Temptation can spring from our own sinful nature and from a love for the world, but as theologian Don Campbell asserts, "Both the Old and New Testaments make it clear that the ultimate source of temptation to sin is Satan."[8]

I've got news for you: Satan is a liar. In fact, the Bible even calls him the "father of lies" (see John 8:44). Everything Satan promises isn't everything he will deliver.

Remember Sergio from the beginning of this chapter? Satan promised him sexual satisfaction and fulfillment through the temptation of a sexually explicit video. Instead, Satan delivered a lifestyle of addiction, loneliness, unquenchable desire, and shame. That's Satan's method of operation, the one he's been using since the beginning of time. In used-car lingo, it's the old "bait and switch" strategy. Promise one thing, but deliver another. Tell half the truth ("It's brand-new!"), but deliver the disappointing, whole truth ("Of course, it doesn't have an engine. . .").

A movie that demonstrates this point in a funny, yet surprisingly accurate manner is the comedy *Bedazzled*. This film stars Brendan Fraser as a hapless soul named Elliot Richards, and Elizabeth Hurley as the sexy, sultry devil. The devil (Hurley) tempts Elliot (Fraser) with a promise to grant seven wishes—in exchange for his soul. I enjoyed this movie first because it definitely made me laugh but also because it unwittingly depicts Satan in the most realistic way I've seen in years.

You see, Satan won't often tempt us in *The Exorcist* style, with ghastly scenes of violence and gruesome, grisly encounters. Most often he'll approach us like Hurley does in *Bedazzled,* as a beautiful, seductive, downright friendly being who seems to have only our best interests at heart.

At the beginning of the movie, Satan is tempting Elliot, trying to convince him to enter into her little soul-for-seven-wishes deal. As part of the temptation, she whisks him off to a fancy nightclub—her nightclub, the DV8. It's late at night, and Elliot is greeted at the door by dozens of adoring "fans," including paparazzi, fashionistas, and more. Inside, the lights and images of the club are colorful and enticing. The place is packed with happy, glamorous people dancing and laughing and carrying on—and they all treat Elliot as if he's some kind of super-celebrity. Beautiful models are flirting with him; successful-looking men are admiring him. He's the star of this show, and Satan has orchestrated it all.

As the movie progresses, Satan's true nature is gradually revealed through a series of deceptions that wreak comedic havoc in Elliot's life, until finally, Elliot has had enough. Looking to confront Satan, our hero makes his way back to that hot spot of a nightclub, this time early in the day.

When Elliot enters the DV8 during the light of day, the truth becomes rancidly clear. Those beautiful, previously sexy dancers are actually fat, old women who've now collapsed in drunken stupors onstage. The successful-looking men are really ragged, worn-out guys who look worse than tired; they look like shallow, defeated people who are simply deluding themselves into thinking they're not. The glamour and excitement from before is now just a trashy, downtrodden room with broken lights and broken people littered among the broken glass. And the devil who was formerly Elliot's best friend? Now she's merely a ravenous beast intent on consuming his soul by any means necessary.

And so the truth comes out. Elliot's temptation to partner with Satan had looked so enticing at first, but in the end it was all just a lie— and a trap.

And that's the way it is for you and me, as well. Satan may come to us with all sorts of attractive temptations—more money, more power, more prestige, more fulfillment, more whatever! But in the end, it's always a lie. What else can we expect from the father of lies?

GOD DOES NOT LEAVE US DEFENSELESS AGAINST TEMPTATION

Here's the good news: The lure of Satan's seemingly irresistible lies is not a hook we have to bite! In 1 Corinthians 10:13 (NLT), the apostle Paul tells us:

But remember that the temptations that come into your life are no different from

what others experience. And God is faith-
ful. He will keep the temptation from
becoming so strong that you can't stand
up against it. When you are tempted, he
will show you a way out so that you will
not give in to it.

Yes, temptation will come. But God, in His great faithfulness, has given us tools to help us—tools that not only keep us from being led *into* temptation but can (by God's grace) lead us *through* temptation to victory on the other side. Let me point out just three of those tools for you here.

1. *Scripture*

If you read the account of Jesus' temptation in Matthew chapter 4 (and I hope you do), one thing immediately stands out: the use of Scripture in the face of temptation. Three times Satan tempted Christ to disobey God, and all three times Jesus' response was simply to speak the words of Scripture right into Satan's face. The result? The devil finally ran away with his proverbial pointed tail tucked between his legs. Nothing he could do could stand against the Word of God!

Why is that? I have a theory. You see, when Christ spoke the words of Scripture, He did more than just quote a few Bible verses; He proclaimed the truth. How can you argue with the truth? In the face of a reality, it's idiotic to keep talking about an unreality.

The only thing necessary for the triumph of evil is for good men to do nothing.

GERMAN CHEMIST, KURT ALDER

Here's what I mean. Let's suppose I come to you today and say, "There is no such thing as the sun. It doesn't exist." Does that tempt you to disbelieve the truth? Of course not. You've seen the sun, felt its warmth on your skin, smelled its life in the very air you breathe. The truth is, the sun exists. And if the sun is shining over my shoulder when I try to convince you it doesn't exist, all you have to do is point—and my little charade is exposed.

Such is the case with the temptation of Christ. Satan tried to camouflage the truth, but he was unable to do so because Jesus pointed to the truth with every Scripture He spoke! We would be wise to learn from His example.

2. *Common Sense*

A second tool we have to combat temptation is run-of-the-mill, everyday, ordinary common sense. I love how authors Bruce & Stan explain this. They say:

> *Sometimes [yielding to temptation] is just a matter of plain stupidity. We stupidly put ourselves in the path of temptation when we could have avoided it altogether.*
>
> *Start being smart about resisting temptation. If you know that you are having difficulty with a particular sin, then arrange the circumstances of your life so that you aren't confronted with the temptation as often. Decide ahead of time what you won't do, where you won't go, and what you won't watch. You might even have to disassociate with a few "friends" who are leading you into trouble.*
>
> *The hardest time to resist temptation is when you're knee-deep in it. It's just a lot easier to stay away from it to begin with.*[9]

You and I must realize that sin is an addiction we all have. Like the recovering alcoholic who determines no longer to visit a bar, we must learn to use common sense to avoid placing ourselves in situations that weaken our resolve to stand firm in God's standards for our lives.

3. Other Christians

Thank God we aren't required to live this Christian life in a vacuum! God has placed us in a family—His family—and we can draw strength from our family members to help us overcome the temptations Satan throws our way.

It's the teamwork principle: We trust in God to lead us away from temptation, and He places us in a "team"—a community of Christians that helps us resist temptation in such a way that our victory becomes more than we could ever accomplish on our own. But it requires that we trust both God and those "teammates" He has placed in our lives.

Wayne Cordiero, pastor of a church in Hilo, Hawaii, learned this principle firsthand through a boat race over the waters of the Pacific Ocean. With his permission, I'll let him tell you about that experience here:

> *One of the more popular sports on the islands is canoe paddling. In this sport, there are six paddlers in a canoe, or* wa`a, *which has a balancing arm called an* ama. *Although navigating one of these ancient canoes may look basic, the technique required is much more than meets the eye.*
>
> *A few summers ago, six of us from the church were invited to compete as a*

crew in an upcoming canoe race. We were game for something new, so we accepted and immediately sought out one of the canoe instructors from a nearby club for a few lessons. We started our first lesson in an adjacent lake of brackish water. Our instructor, Russell Chin, sat astride the nose of the canoe, facing us as he called out signals and instructions.

We were in our places, and the first lesson began.

"OK, everyone!" he yelled. "This is how you hold a paddle," he said, modeling the correct form. As we were figuring out which end we were to grasp and with which hand, he continued.

"We're going to paddle our first stretch of water. It will be an eighth-of-a-mile sprint. When I begin the stopwatch and say 'go,' just paddle as fast and hard as you can. When we cross the finish line, I'll notify you. That's when you can stop paddling. Got it?"

How hard can this be? *I thought.* Even women paddle canoes. This ought to be a breeze! *Just then, my self-confident thoughts were shattered by the sharp call of our coach.*

"Ho`omakaukau? I mua!"

In English, it means, "Ready? Go forward!"

With our muscles bulging and sinews stretched, we burst out of our dead-in-the-water starting position like a drowning elephant trying to get air. We thrashed the water with our paddles on either side of the canoe. Not knowing when to switch from one side to the other, we all figured the best time would simply be when one arm got tired. So, firing at will, I crossed the blade of my oar over and across the canoe, and when I did, I scraped the back of my fellow paddler, Roy Pua-Kaipo, seated directly in front of me. He grunted as my oar etched an unmistakable red mark across his spine. But Roy didn't stop. He just kept beating the water like a trooper. We were on a crusade!

It felt as if hours had transpired. My arms became like lead, and my lungs were on fire. Roy's back was starting to bleed, and our canoe was half filled with water. The elephant was beginning to drown when we finally heard Russell yell, "OK, stop!"

Thank God! *I thought. We abandoned the sinking canoe and let our bodies slump into the water, totally exhausted.*

"One minute, forty-two seconds," Russell called. *"Pretty sad!"*

Like war-torn warriors, we comforted each other, apologizing for the scrapes and wounds inflicted by our flailing paddles. We started bailing the water out of the canoe, which had begun to resemble a defeated submarine more than a sleek racing vessel.

Russell gathered us whimpering novices together, and after sharing a few basics about safety, he taught us how to paddle as a team. Each fledgling paddler was to mirror the one in front of him and everyone in time with the lead stroker. He taught us how to switch our paddles to the opposite hand without injuring each other. We practiced together again and again until our stroking became as rhythmic as a metronome. We were beginning to look good! After a few more practice runs, our coach took us back to our original starting position.

"All right," said Russell, "let's try that same eighth-mile stretch again! Only this time, I want you to stroke as if you were taking a leisurely stroll through the park. No sprinting. Just mirror the one in front of you and switch with a smooth cadence

of rhythm, just as you were taught! Stroke as a team and don't try to break any sound barriers this time, OK?"

With new confidence, we took our mark. Russell barked out the starting signal. "Ho`omakaukau? I mua!"

Our oars silently entered the water, coordinated in perfect time. Mike Diaz, the lead stroker, called out his command, "Hut!" In perfect chorus, we answered, "Ho!" and we were off.

Our canoe cut through the water like a knife through jelly. We switched sides without skipping a beat. We each mirrored the rower in front of us. We were being transformed from a drowning circus animal into a precision machine! Then, just as we were feeling the exhilaration of smooth progress, Russell yelled, "OK! Stop paddling!"

The ahead-of-expected arrival caught us all by surprise.

"Anybody tired?"

We all shook our heads, "No!"

Russell held up his stopwatch so we could see, then exclaimed, "You bested your last time by twenty-four seconds!"

I couldn't believe it! Nobody was injured! No one went overboard out of *sheer exhaustion! No canoe deluged with water! No fire in my lungs! It was a sheer delight! We congratulated each other, gave a few victory shouts, exchanged leis, and took pictures. This was amazing!*

And we did it together! We paddled as a team.[10]

As you and I face our daily struggles against the temptations Satan puts before us, let's be like Wayne Cordiero and his companions, working together and supporting each other to follow our leader to heights that are greater than we can imagine!

THE GREATEST TEMPTATION

Now, as we near the end of both this chapter and this book, I feel it important to share with you what is sometimes my greatest temptation—and one that I'm guessing may be yours as well.

Sometimes the greatest temptation is to do nothing at all.

Too often we focus so much of our strength on what we do, and in doing that we neglect to consider what it is we don't do. As the apostle James said, "Anyone, then, who knows the good he ought to do and doesn't do it, sins" (James 4:17 NIV).

We see a need yet refuse to meet it. We are given an opportunity yet pass because we're just too busy. We are frustrated by the moral decline of our society, so we abandon our efforts to reach out and sit securely in a comfort zone of church attendance and absentee lifestyles while many around us are literally going to hell.

This is something Chuck Colson calls, "Our Comfortable Temptation." Listen to what he said about it in a 1999 commencement speech he gave at Gordon-Conwell Theological Seminary:

> *Just think about the current opportunity before all of us as Christians. . . . All of our civilization is impacted by Christian truth handed down through the centuries, and we are celebrating two thousand years. Yet there are Christians among us saying, "Give up on the culture. Don't worry about it. Just go build up our churches." It is a comfortable message, but it is dead wrong, because this ought to be the time when we as jubilant Christians proclaim truth to the world because the world is hungering to hear it. Why is it wrong for us to withdraw?*

It is tempting, of course. It happened to the church earlier in the century. We withdrew; we built our own churches. . . but never forget that the whole world has been given to us by God. We need to think of the entire world, not just of our own churches and filling our own pews.

No. Withdrawing from the world is wrong for three reasons:

First, I sense that the desire to withdraw is rooted in despair. People are saying, "Let's give up. So many of the battles in the cultural wars have failed; Christian moralistic crusades have failed." But I say, "No. Do not give up, because despair is a sin; it is a sin because it denies the sovereignty of God. . . ."

Second, it is a mistake to withdraw, because biblically we are told that the entire world is the Lord's. Consider Psalm 8, among others. . . . When Abraham Kuyper dedicated the Free University in Holland, he said: "There is not one square inch in the whole domain of our human existence over which Christ, who is sovereign over all, does not cry out, 'Mine!' " It is all God's! . . . We aren't just to be concerned with ourselves. We are to be concerned with the entire world.

Third, to run away now from the
battle of bringing Christian truth to bear
on our culture would be to sound the
defeat at the very time when victory is in
our grasp. . . . This is no time to be talk-
ing about withdrawal and defeat,
because moral discourse is changing in
America. People are coming alive to the
realization that something is wrong. . . .[11]

Let me close this chapter with one more story to illustrate this point for you. I must warn you, it's a true story. And it's about fine, upstanding, churchgoing Christians just like you and me.

This one takes place in Germany during the 1940s, when Adolf Hitler and his Nazi war machine ruled half the world.

But this story isn't about Hitler so much as it's about a man and the little church he attended each week with his friends and neighbors. A German, he considered himself a good Christian, honest in business, charitable in life. Like his countrymen, he had heard stories about what the Nazis were doing to the Jews—rounding them up, imprisoning them in concentration camps, committing mass murders of unwanted people. Yet, he says, "We tried to distance ourselves from it, because, what could anyone do to stop it?"

Running behind the church this man attended was a railroad track, and each Sunday during worship service every parishioner could hear the train's whistle and then the *clack-clack* of its wheels as it passed by. At some point during the war, they began to hear more than just the train going by. They heard human cries for help floating from the cargo holds on the train. Week after week they heard them, until they finally realized that each Sunday train was carrying Jews like cattle to their likely deaths in concentration camps at the end of the line.

Decades later, this nameless German man described his church's response to the calls for help that came past their church each week. Listen to what he said:

> Week after week the whistle would blow. We dreaded to hear the sound of those wheels because we knew that we would hear the cries of the Jews en route to the death camp. Their screams tormented us.
> We knew the time the train was coming, and when we heard the whistle blow we began singing hymns. By the time the train came past our church we were singing at the top of our voices. If we heard the screams, we sang more loudly, and soon we heard them no more.

*Years have passed, and no one talks
about it anymore. But I still hear that
train whistle in my sleep. God forgive me;
forgive all of us who called ourselves
Christians and yet did nothing. . . .*[12]

Though we may be guilty of many things in this life, let us not be guilty of giving in to this greatest temptation—the temptation to do nothing. No, we may not be able to change the sinful policies of our governments, but we can be diligent to pray for God to make that change. No, we may not be able to solve overwhelming crises like homelessness or racism or violent crime, but we can help the person next door to us to live life just a little better than before. No, we may not be able to do everything, but we can—we must— do something.

"And do not lead us into temptation, but deliver us from the evil one," Christ prayed for us. Let us now determine to put feet to that prayer and refuse to give in to Satan's desire for Christians simply to do nothing.

FOR FURTHER REFLECTION. . .

[Jesus said,] "Keep alert and pray. Otherwise temptation will overpower you. For though the spirit is willing enough, the body is weak!"

MATTHEW 26:41 NLT

When people are tempted, they should not say, "God is tempting me." Evil cannot tempt God, and God himself does not tempt anyone. But people are tempted when their own evil desire leads them away and traps them. This desire leads to sin, and then the sin grows and brings death.

JAMES 1:13–15 NCV

I have hidden your word in my heart that I might not sin against you.

PSALM 119:11 NIV

AFTERWORD

Well, that concludes our little exploration of the prayer of Jesus. I want to thank you for being willing to join me on this journey through Matthew 6:9–13. I've treasured our time together.

I want to also let you know that, although the earliest manuscripts of the Gospel of Matthew don't include it, scholars believe that a benedictory phrase was later added to this prayer and attributed to Jesus. (Since prayers like this were often used in a liturgical setting, adding a benediction was a common Jewish custom of that time.) Did Christ actually say those words? It's possible, and some would even argue it to be likely. But because there is uncertainty regarding the origin of that benediction, I've chosen not to devote a chapter to it in this book.

Still, I believe those words are worth sharing with you now. They are:

For Yours is the kingdom and the power and the glory forever. Amen!

It's my prayer that, in some small way, this little book has accomplished that sentiment. It's my hope that through the words you've read in this book, God has been glorified, both in your reading and in your life.

Now, I have one more favor to ask of you. If this book has been meaningful for you, if you were encouraged by something you read here, would you do something for me?

Please share it with someone else.

I'd like to ask you not to let this little tome sit on your shelf gathering dust. Instead, when you are finished with it, pass it on to a friend or family member or neighbor or coworker or anyone else you think might be encouraged by it. I would be honored if you'd share this book with another in that way. Thank you.

And so we end our time together, and as we do, let's both challenge each other to live out the heart behind the words in the prayer of Jesus—today, tomorrow, and for a lifetime.

I'd love to hear from you. You can e-mail me through the "Contact Us" page on my website at: www.Nappaland.com

God bless!

ENDNOTES

CHAPTER 1

1. "What's in a Name," excerpted from *The 1995–1996 Student Plan-It Calendar* by Mike & Amy Nappa (Loveland, Colo.: Group Publishing, 1995). Reprinted with permission.

2. John Trent, *Choosing to Live the Blessing* (Colorado Springs, Colo: WaterBrook, 1997), p. 91.

3. Richard A. Steele Jr. and Evelyn Stoner, ed., *Heartwarming Bible Illustrations* (Chattanooga, Tenn.: AMG Publishers, 1998), p. 169.

4. John Eades, excerpted from *Miracle on Boswell Road* (Uhrichsville, Ohio: Promise Press, 2000). Reprinted with permission.

5. As quoted by Charles R. Swindoll in *The Tale of the Tardy Oxcart* (Nashville, Tenn.: Word, 1998), pp. 80–81.

6. Swindoll, p. 80.

7. Ibid.

8. Trent, pp. 126–127.

CHAPTER 2

1. Larry Libby, *Someday Heaven,* quoted in *The Book of Wisdom* (Sisters, Oreg.: Multnomah, 1997), p. 554.

2. Mary and Bill Barbour, with Rebekah Rendall Blanda, *What Kids Say About Life, Love, and God* (Uhrichsville, Ohio: Promise Press, 2001), pp. 162–164.

3. Bruce Bickel and Stan Jantz, from *Keeping God in the Small Stuff* (Uhrichsville, Ohio: Promise Press, 2000). Reprinted with permission.

4. Joseph Cardinal Bernardin. *The Gift of Peace,* quoted

in *The Book of Wisdom* (Sisters, Oreg.: Multnomah, 1997), pp. 558–559.

5. See 1 Corinthians 15:51–55 in the Bible for more on this.

6. See 1 Kings 8:27 and Psalm 139:7–12 in the Bible for more on this.

7. Ron Rhodes, *Miracles Around Us* (Eugene, Oreg.: Harvest House, 2000). Used by permission.

CHAPTER 3

1. For facts about General Hooker see "Joseph Hooker Source Page," About.com website address: http://americanhistory.about.com/gi/dynamic/off-site.htm?site=http%3A%2F%2Fwww.aotc.net%2FHooker_home.htm; and "Hooker." Wilton's Word and Phrase Origins website address: http://www.wordorigins.org/wordorh.htm#hooker.

2. This material is drawn from Ken Hemphill, *The Names of God* (Nashville, Tenn.: Broadman & Holman, 2001), pp. 63–78, 49, 85, 161, 177, 91, 35, 5, 4.

3. Jim Burns and Greg Mckinnon, *Illustrations, Stories, and Quotes* (Ventura, Calif.: Gospel Light, 1997), pp. 143–144.

4. From *"Talk and the Voice of the Martyrs," Jesus Freaks* (Tulsa, Okla.: Asbury, 1999), pp. 50–51.

CHAPTER 4

1. John E. McFadyen, *The Prayers of the Bible* (Chattanooga, Tenn.: AMG Publishers, 1995), pp. 103–104. Originally published in 1906 by Hodder & Stoughton in London.

2. George Thomas Kurian, ed., *Nelson's New Christian Dictionary* (Nashville, Tenn.: Thomas Nelson, 2001), p. 428.

3. See Revelation 21 in the Bible.

4. "The Angel of Antietam" adapted and reprinted from *Life Lessons from America's Civil War* by Mike Nappa and Dick Olson. Copyright © 1999 by Nappaland Communications, Inc. and Dick Olson. Originally published on Nappaland.com "The Free Webzine for Families." Used by permission. All rights reserved.

5. Dave & Neta Jackson, *Hero Tales,* Volume IV (Minneapolis, Minn.: Bethany, 2001), pp. 11–13.

6. David Wardell and Jeffrey Leever, *Daily Disciples* (Uhrichsville, Ohio: Promise Press, 2001). Used with permission.

7. Anne Gordon, *A Book of Saints* (New York: Bantam, 1994), pp. 75–81.

8. Christopher L. Coppernoll, *Soul 2 Soul* (Nashville, Tenn.: Word, 1998), pp. 162–164.

9. "An Angel's Dress" is excerpted from *Miracle on Boswell Road,* by John Eades (Uhrichsville, Ohio: Promise Press, 2000). Reprinted with permission.

CHAPTER 5

1. Charles R. Swindoll, *The Tale of the Tardy Oxcart* (Nashville, Tenn.: Word, 1998), p. 247.

2. Wayne A. Detzler, *New Testament Words in Today's Language* (Wheaton, Ill.: Victor, 1986), p. 394.

3. Selwyn Hughes, *Prayer, the Greatest Power* (Nashville, Tenn.: Broadman & Holman, 2001), pp. 30–31.

4. Ray Pritchard, *FAQ* (Nashville, Tenn.: Broadman & Holman, 2001), p. 67.

5. See Romans 8:29–30 in the Bible for more on this.

6. Larry Shallenberger "The Holy Arsonist," *Children's Ministry Magazine* (Loveland, Colo.: Group Publishing, 2000). Reprinted by permission.

7. A.W. Tozer, *The Knowledge of the Holy* (San Francisco: Harper & Row, 1961), pp. 63–64.

8. Swindoll, p. 245.

9. Yogi Berra, *When You Come to a Fork in the Road, Take It!* (New York: Hyperion, 2001), pp. 111–112.

10. Wayne Rice, *Hot Illustrations for Youth Talks* (El Cajon, Calif.: Youth Specialties, 1994), p. 220.

CHAPTER 6

1. Bruce E. Olsen, *Bruchko* (Altamonte Springs, Fla.: Creation House, 1973), pp. 89–90.

2. See Exodus 16:1–31 in the Bible for more on this.

3. John E. McFadyen, *The Prayers of the Bible* (Chattanooga, Tenn.: AMG Publishers, 1995), p. 104. Originally published in 1906 by Hodder & Stoughton in London.

4. Ralph Gower, *The New Manners and Customs of Bible Times* (Chicago, Ill.: Moody, 1987), p. 36.

5. As quoted by Selwyn Hughes in *God the Enough* (Nashville, Tenn.: Broadman & Holman, 2001), p. 7.

6. Dave and Neta Jackson, *Hero Tales,* Volume III (Minneapolis, Minn.: Bethany, 1998), pp. 38–39.

7. Edward K. Rowell, ed., *Fresh Illustrations for Preaching and Teaching* (Grand Rapids, Mich.: Baker, 1997), p. 210.

8. This book was titled *True Stories of Answered Prayer* and was published by Tyndale House in 1999.

9. From a 1998 Nappaland Communications Inc. interview with Terri Blackstock.

10. Kelly Kurt, "Prom Belles Emerge from Rubble" (The Associated Press), *Orlando Reporter-Herald,* 8 May 1999, p. D-5.

CHAPTER 7

1. The letters to and from God that open this chapter are excerpted from Philis Boultinghouse, *Heavenly Mail* (West Monroe, La.: Howard, 2001). Reprinted with permission. Scriptures sources used as the basis for "A Letter from Heaven" are: John 3:16; Jeremiah 33:8; 2 Chronicles 7:14; Psalms 65:3; 85:2; Romans 8:31–34; 3:22–24; 1 John 1:9, 8, 10; Ephesians 1:7; Hebrews 9:22; Matthew 6:14–15; Luke 6:37.

2. Don Campbell, Wendell Johnston, John Walvoord, and John Witmer, *The Theological Wordbook* (Nashville, Tenn.: Word, 2000), p. 131.

3. See 1 John 2:1–2 for more on this.

4. Dave and Neta Jackson, *Hero Tales*, Volume II (Minneapolis, Minn.: Bethany, 1997), pp. 105–106, 113–114.

5. See Luke 19:1–10 in the Bible for more on Zacchaeus.

6. Richard A. Steele Jr. and Evelyn Stoner, *Heartwarming Bible Illustrations* (Chattanooga, Tenn.: AMG Publishers, 1998), p. 150.

7. As quoted by Wayne A. Detzler in *New Testament Words in Today's Language* (Wheaton, Ill.: Victor, 1986), p. 169.

8. Detzler, p. 169.

9. Steele and Stoner, p. 224.

10. The story about Vaclav Maly is excerpted from *Chuck Colson Speaks* (Uhrichsville, Ohio: Promise Press, 2000). Reprinted with permission.

Chapter 8

1. Barry Cadish, *Damn! Reflections on Life's Biggest Regrets* (Kansas City, Mo.: Andrews McMeel Publishing, 2001), p. 79.

2. "The Hall of Fakes," *Sports Illustrated,* 2 July 2001,
p. 26.

3. Don Campbell, Wendell Johnston, John Walvoord,
and John Witmer, *The Theological Wordbook*
(Nashville, Tenn.: Word, 2000), p. 347.

4. See Genesis 3 in the Bible for more on this.

5. Henry Clarence Thiessen, *Introductory Lectures in
Systematic Theology* (Grand Rapids, Mich.: Wm. B.
Eerdmans, 1966) p. 254.

6. Ray Pritchard. *FAQ* (Nashville, Tenn.: Broadman &
Holman, 2001), pp. 94–95, 93.

7. See Matthew 4:1–11 in the Bible for more on this.

8. Campbell, p. 347. Also, see Genesis 3; Job 1:6–2:10;
1 Corinthians 7:5; 1 Thessalonians 3:5; 1 Peter
5:8–9; and Revelation 2:10 in the Bible for more
on this.

9. Bruce Bickel and Stan Jantz, *Keeping God in the Small
Stuff* (Uhrichsville, Ohio: Promise Press, 2000).

10. The canoe-racing story is excerpted from *Doing
Church as a Team* by Wayne Cordeiro (Ventura,
Calif.: Gospel Light/Regal Books, 2000).
Used with permission.

11. "Our Comfortable Temptation" excerpted from
Chuck Colson Speaks by Charles W. Colson
(Uhrichsville, Ohio: Promise Press, 2001).
Reprinted with permission.

12. Erwin W. Lutzer, *Hitler's Cross* (Chicago, Ill.:
Moody, 1995), pp. 99–100.

ABOUT THE AUTHOR

Mike Nappa is an award-winning and best-selling author of many books, including: *A Heart Like His; Who Moved My Church?* and *The Courage to Be Christian.* He's also a prolific writer who has published hundreds of articles in numerous publications like *HomeLife, CCM, FaithWorks, Focus on the Family* (Growing Years Edition), *Christian Single, Breakaway, Brio, Campus Life, Christian Parenting Today, ParentLife, Stand Firm,* Christianity.com, Crosswalk.com, CBN.com, and more.

Additionally, Mike is the creator and publisher of the award-winning web site, Nappaland.com, "The Free Webzine for Families," and creator of Focus on the Family Clubhouse's award-winning children's comic, Johnny Grav & The Visioneer.

A former youth pastor, Mike studied theology and Christian education at Biola University and now makes his home in Colorado where he is active in his church.

To contact Mike, access his free webzine for families at: www.Nappaland.com

Inspirational Library

Beautiful purse/pocket-size editions of Christian classics bound in flexible leatherette. These books make thoughtful gifts for everyone on your list, including yourself!

When I'm on My Knees　　The highly popular collection of devotional thoughts on prayer, especially for women.
　　Flexible Leatherette. $4.97

The Bible Promise Book　　Over 1,000 promises from God's Word arranged by topic. What does God promise about matters like: Anger, Illness, Jealousy, Love, Money, Old Age, and Mercy? Find out in this book!
　　Flexible Leatherette. $3.97

Daily Wisdom for Women　　A daily devotional for women seeking biblical wisdom to apply to their lives. Scripture taken from the New American Standard Version of the Bible.
　　Flexible Leatherette. $4.97

My Daily Prayer Journal　　Each page is dated and features a Scripture verse and ample room for you to record your thoughts, prayers, and praises. One page for each day of the year.
　　Flexible Leatherette. $4.97

Available wherever books are sold.
Or order from:

Barbour Publishing, Inc.
P.O. Box 719
Uhrichsville, OH 44683
http://www.barbourbooks.com

If you order by mail, add $2.00 to your order for shipping.
Prices are subject to change without notice.